NAVIGATING THE CAREGIVER RIVER

A JOURNEY
TO SUSTAINABLE
CAREGIVING

THERESA WILBANKS

Copyright © 2022 Theresa Wilbanks.

All rights reserved. No part of this publication may be reproduced, distributed, or transmitted in any form or by any means, including photocopying, recording, or other electronic or mechanical methods, without the prior written permission of the publisher, except in the case of brief quotations embodied in critical reviews and certain other noncommercial uses permitted by copyright law. For permission requests, write to the publisher, addressed "Attention: Permissions Coordinator," at the address below.

ISBN: 978-1-7379821-0-4 (Paperback)
ISBN: 978-1-7379821-1-1 (eBook)

The information in this book is for general information only; please contact your legal or financial advisors or medical provider for guidance on your particular situation.

Front cover image by Damonza
Book design by Damonza

First printing edition 2021.

www.sustainablecaregiving.com

CONTENTS

Introduction 1

Part I: Sustainability Strategies: The Emotions 13

1 Accept & Reframe: Flow with the Current. 15
2 Set, Modify & Maintain Boundaries: Respect the Riverbank 33
3 Cultivate Awareness through Mindfulness: Flow from the Present Moment 45
4 Reimagine Self-Care: Expeditions Require Stamina 61
5 Cultivate Compassion & Forgiveness: Let Love Release the Anchor 85
6 Release the Emotions: Waterfalls Lead to Rainbows . . . 101

Part II: Sustainability Strategies: The Practical 113

7 Timing the Transitions: Read the River 115
8 Have the Conversations: Build your Boat Together . . . 131
9 Hospitalizations Happen - Have a Plan: Multi-day Side Trip Itinerary 151
10 Taking the Wheel: Orient Yourself for the Transition . . 165
11 Oversee Medication Management: Chart a Safe Passage through Prescriptions 175
12 Prepare for Care at Home: Train for Turbulent and Swift Water 191

Acknowledgments 205

In memory of my father who continued to teach me life lessons of courage, hope, and love as we navigated our caregiving journey together.

INTRODUCTION

My caregiving journey started like many others. I did not know that I was a caregiver. I was simply a dutiful daughter doing what I had seen my parents do for their parents. Looking back, well before my husband and I moved back from France to be closer to Dad, I was wading into caregiving, sticking a toe into the waters to check the temperature. From a hotel lobby in the Czech Republic, I listened as Dad shared that a friend had been on his laptop, had his password, and was trying to get him a better deal on health insurance. I called Dad's friend and set clear boundaries with clear consequences around who may have access to Dad's computer and who was authorized to get involved in his medical decisions. I didn't realize that I was advocating and functioning in the role of long-distance caregiver. I was only casually familiar with the concept of boundary setting. In my mind, I was just a protective daughter who was ready to jump on the next flight to Tampa if this person did not get out of Dad's business.

From Wading to Drowning

By the time I connected with the term caregiver, I was drowning and burned-out. What started as running errands and helping with finances turned into a full-time, plus overtime, all-consuming job with no pay, no job description, no authority, and no appreciation. My services were both welcomed by Dad yet rejected as unnecessary because he believed that he was getting by just fine on his own. By the time I realized that my role had a title and my responsibilities could be defined, I was too overwhelmed to manage my job with the level-headedness I had previously possessed in my career. I rode waves of stress and worry of varying intensity throughout the days and nights. My path was not sustainable.

We had been in France for seven years on an open-ended contract. Our return to the US was sparked by a fire in Dad's condo, started when a tray of candles burned through the tray, then his dresser as he napped. He initially downplayed the fire as a minor incident but revealed more details over time. It was clear that we should be closer than an ocean away.

Soon after we moved back, Dad had a stroke. In addition, it was evident to everyone but him that he should no longer drive. Then, his identity was stolen, *twice*. We were confident and grateful that our timing was appropriate. Looking back, I remember helping here and there, and it felt good to be of service. Next, I remember when every waking thought was a worry. I don't remember moving from one state of being to the next. The shift was gradual and likely started soon after the stroke and subsequent confrontations over the keys to the car. The loving, respectful relationship that Dad and I enjoyed began to crumble under this new caregiver, care receiver dynamic that neither of us wanted.

The Caregiver River
I came to see that the caregiving journey was like being in a raft on a river. There were calm sections, then rapids and swift water that knocked me off my feet, waterfalls that I didn't see coming, and obstacles that blocked forward momentum and caused traumatizing frustration. I was frequently tossed out of the raft and underwater. At times, I was out of the raft, scarcely holding on as we bounced from rock to log, at the mercy of the wild current. As I began to manage the experience with more confidence and agility, the river didn't change, but how I navigated the river changed.

When the overwhelm first set in, I could not understand why helping was so hard. None of the tasks or responsibilities were difficult on their own. Yet, feelings of anger, resentment, and guilt swirled like a whirlpool that pulled me under, undermining my confidence, compassion, and core values. As Dad resisted, I insisted. It felt like we were in combat. The conflicts wore down my resilience. I was angry that I was angry. I wanted to navigate this river and steer this raft rather than be tossed around at the mercy of the next clash, resistance, or broken system. Dad and I argued over driving, medication management, ladders, the stove, skydiving, his knee surgery at 97, and even blueberries. While I learned lessons from each of the skirmishes, the blueberry battle was a turning point. It was amazing what havoc could be wrought by a resealable bag of blueberries; I was ready to die on Blueberry Hill. Stepping off the battlefield, I understood more clearly when winning was losing, and I permanently put down the battle armor. I focused on big picture objectives such as maintaining relationships, helping Dad process his history, creating a peaceful environment, and getting to win - win. By releasing control, I gained control and began navigating.

Navigating

I set about dissecting the emotional challenges and studied tactics to counter each one. These tactics became strategies that I subjected to trial and error. The strategies included establishing routines, setting boundaries, cultivating compassion, forgiving myself and others, accepting the role, accepting help, letting go of expectations, and changing how I viewed obstacles. Through this new lens of acceptance, I discovered when losing was winning. A shift in perspective swung my attitude from frustrated to empowered. When we faced a new obstacle, I viewed it as an opportunity to improve our situation.

Sometimes the obstacle is in the way, and sometimes the obstacle is the way. Is it stopping us or showing us which way to go?

RYAN HOLIDAY,
THE OBSTACLE IS THE WAY

Appreciating that we grow stronger as we navigate our caregiving journey, I recognized that within each struggle, I had the opportunity to develop skills and perspectives that would help now and beyond caregiving. The challenge was to pace myself, figure out what worked, and then figure it out again as the circumstances changed. I explored self-care and how it fit into this new reality. Journaling and counseling became my methods of venting. I replaced my non-strategy of wondering and worrying about what was around the next bend with creating an itinerary, planning, and preparing for the future.

A Sustainable Caregiving Foundation

As I continued to learn more about each strategy to manage stress, I combined the strategies. When the strategies began to work together, they began to work. Because challenges and needs were fluid and changed from day to day, sometimes from hour to hour, strategies and solutions had to be fluid. What worked one day to manage stress or circumstances didn't always work the next day. As I learned to modify my core set of strategies to fit the current situation, I was able to make the adjustments more quickly. The fluid-meets-solid, sustainable caregiving foundation for well-being was formed. The journey became an adventure, a meaningful pilgrimage, and a rite of passage.

I organized self-care activities, including sleep, nutrition, meditation, and exercise, into routines. I set boundaries to protect the routines. These combined strategies allowed me to focus on my well-being which replenished my compassion reserves and restored my capacity for compassion. When I reconnected to compassion, it was like putting on glasses with a new prescription, but instead of seeing things clearly again, I was *feeling* things clearly again. I found previously elusive gratitude. Forgiveness freed up my thoughts to focus on love. Meditation and exercise left me feeling refreshed, reenergized, and at peace rather than frazzled and frustrated when I could not calm the negative thoughts. I found a counselor who was a good fit, and I felt empowered by the sessions rather than suffering from a vulnerability hangover[1] from the lack of validation. I looked for more ways to accept help and used the added time to focus on my well-being. Walking the path with folks who could share the load literally and figuratively lightened the burden and offered gifts to everyone involved.

---

1 Brené Brown, "Listening to Shame," *TED2012* video, 00.06. March 2012, https://www.ted.com/talks/brene_brown_listening_to_shame/transcript?language=en

Parting

The strategies helped me navigate, but the caregiver river continued to flow, and obstacles and challenges were around each bend. Dad's increasing anxiety over the progression of his lung disease became all-consuming and began to take over my thoughts as well as his. I worried about him worrying. I realized he needed help, and I needed to learn new skills and set emotional boundaries. I contacted our hospice social worker, and we came up with a plan. We organized a visitor to answer his questions and listen to his concerns. I learned how to engage with Dad to validate his fears and then turn his attention to other topics.

Dad passed suddenly, six weeks after his 99th birthday. An avid painter, he was painting the afternoon before he died. He enjoyed his 3pm gin while we chatted. Our afternoon sessions allowed us to step back into our father-daughter roles, where Dad relayed memories from his days at sea during WWII or his life growing up on a farm. The morning that he passed, Dad made his bed and made his morning coffee. He watched mass, and then we switched the station to his favorite music, big band. My husband and I could see that Dad was in distress. The nurse came. Dad thought he was just having a bad day. Many months before, when I asked Dad what he would consider a good death, he replied, "Dying in my sleep." That's not how it was meant to be, and I will forever be grateful that we had this last morning with Dad and thankful that we were with him when he transitioned.

We are all on a journey to a common destination, end-of-life, and we were helping Dad, who was further along on his journey. This perspective helped me pivot mid-journey to maximize memories and, in the process, minimize stress and regret and create a more meaningful experience for all of us. Now, that was win - win.

Your journey

Like me, you might be asking yourself, "How long can I keep doing this?" Sustainable caregiving is about developing the strategies necessary for you as the caregiver to continue to provide care to your family member as long as required. Sustainable caregiving will look different for everyone but has one thing in common: Sustainability will enable you to continue to have a good quality of life when competing priorities conspire to place your needs last. For example, transitions come fast and furious, and while you may not know what is around the next bend, a stable foundation of strategies will help you navigate the transitions with confidence.

Sustainability requires that we manage legal matters and financial resources, which may be limited when the time we spend caregiving is time spent away from a career. We can identify the activities that help us stay healthy and thrive: exercising, spending time in nature, reading, listening to music, or watching a favorite show. Our physical and emotional well-being benefit from taking time to do what makes us feel alive, feel whole and feel different from how we feel when we are in our caregiving role. Just taking time to breathe can feel like an indulgence when we are navigating rapids without a raft. Yet, these simple pleasures that reconnect us to ourselves are crucial to finding and appreciating calm waters.

Validation and empathy
Being a caregiver is lonely. We are often isolated from friends because we are too busy to join them, and they genuinely don't understand the stress. Trying to explain what we are going through is like trying to explain why we don't like a particular food. If the listener can't relate, they can be a bit judgy. Often, not even our health care professionals get it. A doctor, when I shared that I was stressed due to Dad's willful ways, asked, "Can't you just let it roll off your back?" My therapist, who I was seeing due to caregiver stress, asked, "You do know that you are in this situation because you choose to be?". I say asked, but these were rhetorical questions without any attempt to understand my experience. If we can't receive compassion from those paid to look after our well-being, then it is no wonder that our friends and family members struggle to offer us the validation and empathy we desperately need.

Lessons learned
Along the journey, I learned that it is not possible to exert control over the uncontrollable. The constant effort is self-defeating and unsustainable. Asking for help is a

sign of strength rather than weakness. Acceptance leads to sustainability. Acceptance includes acceptance of the situation, acceptance of limitations (yours and others), acceptance of the systems, loss, help. Time away to recharge is crucial. It might have been anything from a morning run to a weekend music festival, but looking forward to something meaningful kept my head above water. Making time to enjoy a bit of the previous relationship we had as father and daughter was challenging but well worth the effort. Caregiving can be sustainable with the right tools, strategies, and support.

Book Organization
This book is divided into two parts. In Part 1, I share the six strategies that helped calm the emotional storms. These strategies include acceptance, setting boundaries, cultivating, and practicing mindfulness and compassion, with an emphasis on self-compassion. Also included are re-defining self-care, journaling, establishing routines, and how to create a support system by combining the strategies that work for you. A caregiver support system integrates your values with activities that support those values. The support system sustains you on your caregiving journey. Just like rivers are managed with dams, riverbank reinforcements, and reservoirs to support irrigation and prevent flooding, erosion, and the build-up of sediment; we can manage our environment by establishing a system of protections that support our fragile caregiving ecosystem.

To develop your system, determine what components and strategies will help you stay afloat. Which practices keep you moving confidently through the rapids toward calm waters, and which self-care activities calm the inner storms? Trial and error is a necessary part of this process as you assemble your personal support system. Consider setting aside rather than discarding the strategies that do not currently serve you because they may fit in the future. When you have identified the core components and understand how they work, you can observe how they work together in your caregiving environment to provide the best level of support.

In Part 2, I share strategies to manage the more practical matters, such as knowing when to get more involved in care, planning, and preparing for the conversations that create the logistics foundation. The legal, financial, and medical components can be complicated. Discussing end-of-life wishes can be uncomfortable and emotional. Communication about care can quickly become combative. Beginning with the end in mind will help you determine the objectives of your caregiving journey and help you stay focused on the goal so that the collaborative outcomes are win - win. I discuss some of the solutions to the more minor challenges and what it was like to clear the more considerable hurdles, including driving and medication management. I felt like I was dogpaddling in the deep end during the first few hospitalizations and the lessons and strategies learned from the times of crisis were invaluable.

Like paddles that work best when synchronized, the strategies synchronize and work together to support you and your unique circumstances. When the strategies work together, your raft will be stable and move with fluidity and momentum, using the current to navigate obstacles and cruise through the rapids. When the strategies are out of sync, the journey will feel turbulent, and the obstacles will throw you off course.

 Look for this icon for tips on how the strategies connect to help create a fluid yet stable support system.

Your journey to sustainability will look different than mine. Sharing my search for strategies, however, can help you find yours more quickly. My story may offer hope in what can feel like a hopeless situation. The stories and strategies for a sustainable experience apply whether you share a residence with your care recipient or live minutes, or even hours away. I hope that as you stock your life raft with sustainability supplies, you will begin to navigate your journey empowered with skills and purpose. You might even be able to reach over the side and pull another family caregiver on board and help them learn how to navigate the caregiver river.

PART I
SUSTAINABILITY STRATEGIES: THE EMOTIONS

When we are no longer able to change a situation, we are challenged to change ourselves.

VIKTOR FRANKL,
MAN'S SEARCH FOR MEANING

1 ACCEPT & REFRAME: FLOW WITH THE CURRENT

You can't cry it away or eat it away or starve it away or walk it away or punch it away or even therapy it away. It's just there, and you have to survive it. You have to endure it. You have to live through it and love it and move on and be better for it...

– Cheryl Strayed,
Tiny Beautiful Things: Advice on
Love and Life from Dear Sugar

WHEN WE FEEL like we are drowning from caregiving's constant stressors, the overwhelm can distort and sink our thoughts toward the depths of despair. Our situation can feel hopeless, and we can feel helpless. We may harbor an expectation that we should be happy, and the shock of immense, uncomfortable, negative emotions can catch us off guard. We often get caught up in all-or-nothing thinking, placing blame, and focusing on "shoulds," and our resistance to reality wears down our resilience. When we accept our situation and reframe the obstacles that obstruct the flow of our caregiver river, we maintain momentum and balance through the boulders and the rapids. We navigate the waterfalls with confidence. Acceptance and reframing combine and become one single strategy foundational to a sustainable caregiving experience because as we release resistance, we release stress.

Accepting our situation means we recognize that things will not always go according to our expectations. However, we can reframe those expectations. By relinquishing our attempt to control people, processes, and outcomes, we regain control when frustrations no longer have power over our emotions. Acceptance plays a role in turning obstacles into opportunities. When we accept that our path forward has been blocked and we pause to reframe the obstruction, we discover when losing is winning. For example, we have an opportunity to accept broken systems, people within systems, as well as friends and family who let us down. When we chart a new way forward, not just despite the disappointments, but because of them, we are navigating and our path is meaningful, rewarding, and sustainable. Let's look at three facets of acceptance. First, the power of accepting the role and how reframing offers peace and sustainability. Second, let's consider when winning is losing and how accepting and reframing the role's challenges can transform the experience. Third, let's look at how facing an obstacle can feel like losing, but with acceptance and reframing can be a big win in the end.

Accept the Role – It Will Empower You

Resistance to either the caregiving role or responsibilities can cause a great deal of stress. The act of acceptance provides relief. Acceptance is active rather than passive. It requires leaning into negative thoughts and emotions. It is distressing to think that we have taken a wrong turn on life's journey. It is empowering to know that we are on the right path and precisely where we are supposed to be. Accepting our circumstances is like meeting ourselves where we are on the path and moving forward together in agreement rather than a part of you seeking an alternative route, an alternative reality.

Before caregiving, I had never thought of acceptance as a strategy. The first few years that my husband, Joe and I were wading into the caregiving experience, we could continue much of our life as we wished. While I struggled to accept some of the challenges that went along with the caregiving role, I did not feel resistance to the role itself yet. As we began to manage more of Dad's care and our movements became more restricted, I became less tolerant of Dad's insistence that he didn't need help, his resistance to help, and his decisions that I believe demonstrated poor judgment. At one point, I walked in and found him on a 6 ft. ladder attempting to velcro one of his paintings to the ceiling in his bedroom. He repeatedly drove his golf cart to church, crossing a busy road and breaking two laws in the process. He ordered items he saw on TV, and then I was tasked with returning them. He seemed amused by my reactions, further infuriating me. Gradually I began to resist, and eventually I completely resented the role.

Our situation was not sustainable. My emotional state was not sustainable. The more I sought external answers and solutions, the more hopeless I became. The research revealed that Dad's behavior was not an anomaly. My reactions were not unique. I started reading books and seeing a therapist. I joined forums. Searching for the solution to my angst became a part-time job. Many caregivers in the forums felt only gratitude for the opportunity to care for a family member. I could not look to them for direction because from where I was, they were on a different path that was on a distant planet. My resistance to the role of caregiver undermined all my efforts toward creating a sustainable experience. I finally accepted and reframed my role and responsibilities. The solution was hiding in plain sight, under the layers of resentment. Caring for Dad was precisely what I was meant to be doing.

The shift from resistance to acceptance occurred when I came across the concept of "amor fati," which means not just accepting your fate, but loving it. German philosopher Friedrich Nietzsche coined the term, but the idea originated with the Stoics[2]. Nietzsche wrote, *My formula for greatness in a human being is amor fati: that one*

---

[2] Stoicism is a school of philosophy originating from ancient Greece and Rome that taught virtues to minimize negative emotions by focusing on positive emotions.

wants nothing to be different, not forward, not backward, not in all eternity. Not merely bear what is necessary, still less conceal it–all idealism is mendaciousness in the face of what is necessary-but love it.[3] Before acceptance, I could not imagine loving my fate, and because the philosophy felt so extreme, I felt compelled to examine further what I was resisting. I discovered that primarily, I resented the tether that bound my stubborn inner teenager to her stubborn controlling father. Acceptance led me to reframe our experience to serve the bigger picture. Amor Fati became my mantra. "Love your fate" became my mission. This acceptance was a gift of perspective and peace. It kept me from asking, "Why me?" and kept me focused on, "What now?". It drove me to ask the questions, "How can I make the best of this situation?" and "How can I help others who are struggling with similar challenges?" Stoic philosophy helped me connect to my spiritual purpose.

    I let go of the expectation that I was entitled; entitled to happiness, entitled to live a life entirely on my terms. I had accepted the good times without question, so why shouldn't I accept the more challenging episodes? Equally, with a big sigh and a bit of sadness, I accepted impermanence as a purposeful part of life. This was a start, but in the beginning of the revelation and reframing, it still felt passive and like I was giving up. I had to take steps to embrace completely the relationship and role and

---

[3]   Friedrich Nietzsche, *Ecce Homo: How One Becomes What One Is*, (LRP, 2017), Kindle Edition, 25.

relinquish control to find true freedom. To reframe my experience, I directly connected gratitude and caregiving. I wrote out the reasons that our situation was positive, and those reasons for gratitude became my most precious life raft supplies.

As I transferred my rage against reality into loving my fate, I leaned into the emotions. It was an active path to acceptance: accepting the situation, accepting the emotions, accepting help, accepting forgiveness, and accepting loss. And, in this process, I found happiness, joy, a path forward that was sustainable, and a journey that became an adventure.

Eckhart Tolle says that we are aligned with the energy in the universe only when we are in one of three modalities – acceptance, enjoyment, or enthusiasm. He also says that without this alignment, we are creating suffering for ourselves and others.[4] By railing against reality, I had created suffering for myself and others. It was not enough to accept that everything in life can't be fixed. I had to accept that it was never broken.

Chasing elusive acceptance put me in a state of constant low-level anxiety. I was chasing control. I learned that control could not be caught unless it was released. Awareness and communication helped me flip the script from "I have to be a caregiver" to "I get to be a caregiver." As a result, I was more open to what this journey was revealing and was offering.

---

4   Eckhart Tolle, *"A New Earth: Awakening to Your Life's Purpose"*, (Penguin, 2006), 178.

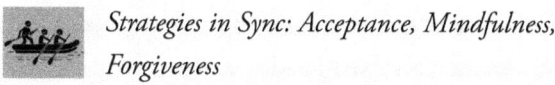 *Strategies in Sync: Acceptance, Mindfulness, Forgiveness*

When we move into the flow of our experience, we can use the strategies to keep our momentum moving with the current.

- Mindfulness: Practicing mindfulness keeps us flowing from the present moment, where awareness will alert us to our resistance to the current and allow us to course-correct our direction and move to a place of acceptance which keeps us flowing with the current.
- Forgiveness: Forgiving ourselves and others releases our thoughts from past grudges so that we can be more mindful and focus on the present moment. Forgiveness helps us stay focused on forward movement and problem solving rather than paddling upstream, focused on resentment.

Reflect

- Is there an aspect of caregiving that you resent or resist? What would happen if you accepted rather than resisted?
- What if you genuinely believed that your current situation is exactly as it is supposed to be? What would you do differently?
- Eckhart Tolle said, "Stress is caused by being 'here' but wanting to be 'there,' or being in the

present but wanting to be in the future. It's a split that tears you apart inside."[5] How does this relate to your experience as a caregiver?

Journal

- Do you feel aligned with acceptance, enjoyment, or enthusiasm? How does your connection or lack of connection to these modes create suffering?
- If you applied the concept of amor fati, love your fate, to caregiving, how would it change the experience for you?
- If impermanence is a part of life, how can you achieve emotional stability?

Practice

- When you feel yourself railing against reality, tune into the source of the resistance. Note the thoughts in your journal.
- Explore the reasons behind the resistance either through reflection or journaling.

When Winning is Losing

While I embraced the role, I knew that much needed to change to sustain my ability to provide care. I analyzed what wasn't working and realized that the frequent bat-

---

5   Eckhart Tolle, *"The Power of Now: A Guide to Spiritual Enlightenment",* (New World Library, 2010) 84.

tles ranging from mini to epic were happening because of my reactions and my resistance to Dad's will. When I saw more clearly that winning an argument was losing our relationship, I reframed the situation by letting go of expectations and perceived control over outcomes.

One of the biggest lessons in letting go of control and accepting that Dad was free to make his own decisions came in the early years of caregiving. Dad wanted to jump out of a plane for his 94th birthday. He brought it up every day with an insistence that triggered my angst. I wasn't sure how serious he was, but it agitated me. He knew it and seemed amused by it. I discouraged, deflected, and resisted. Dad brought it up with his primary care physician, who said, "Why not?" It was one of those rhetorical questions that I could have answered with a monologue, but in shock, I just stammered, "Why not!" My response wasn't a question. It was a way of relenting and releasing. My "Why not?" became "What the heck was all the fuss?".

Back at home, I asked Dad if he wanted me to arrange the jump. His friends and family were not happy. They were where I had been. They had not endured the months of daily drama. I did my best to help them catch up and understand that this was the request of an adult with a reasonably sound mind, and we would appreciate their support.

My brother and his daughter decided to jump with Dad. We met at the location. Dad's friend, Bud, joined to watch. Bud was quite unhappy with me for "allowing" this to proceed and did not hold back, frequently whispering to me that I should put a stop to this madness. That morning Dad tried to back out, but it was scheduled, and I wasn't going to call it off unless we were at the site, and he decided at that moment that he changed his mind. Was this pushback my way of continuing to wrestle for control?

Dad met his jump partner, who said he could land a 94-year-old on his feet. The less risky alternative was to slide in. To me this all still seemed like a terrible idea, but the release forms were completed so we settled in, watching others go up and come down while waiting for Dad's turn. I just wanted it to be over. I got my wish. The last group to land was a team of instructors who said that the winds had become too dangerous to continue. We were welcome to wait and see if things changed. Dad did not want to wait. We could reschedule or get a refund. Dad opted for a refund. His memory of the non-event doesn't include him trying to back out the morning of the jump. He only remembers that the wind foiled his plan, and that is not wrong.

I recalled this multi-month-long battle each time we butted heads in another clash of wills. Many "disagreeable" decisions that Dad had made could have had repercussions for all of us, and this goes along with the caregiving territory. Safety vs. independence can lead to the most epic battles and leave a path of destruction that takes ages to clear. Shed the battle armor, even when your parent wants to jump out of a plane.

Not being in control can be a powerful trigger. The tighter we hold on, the more control we relinquish. Exposing the triggers takes away their power; awareness sheds light on the cause of an overreaction or unnecessary confrontation. Sustainability is only possible when we minimize conflict. This accepting and reframing reality is firmly within our control.

What is the cost of winning vs. the cost of losing? We might win by making our point. But at what cost? We must consider the objectives of our caregiving journey. What is our goal? For our family member to experience peace and feel supported? For us as caregivers to come through the experience healthy and whole? Steven Covey's second habit of highly effective people is to begin with the end in mind.[6] Does winning this battle help you achieve your objectives, or does it derail your momentum? After learning to accept and reframe, I'd ask myself if I was willing to die on whatever hill was the battle of the day. These micro acts of acceptance finally led to the breakthrough that won the war. Life presented a challenge, and I had treated it as a competition with a winner and a loser. I realized that we all won when I fulfilled my role with intention and compassion. This required that I define my intention and goals so that I stayed focused on the ultimate objective.

A meaningful journey was the goal. When I accepted that we were on this end-of-life journey together, I could

---

[6] Stephen R. Covey, *"The Seven Habits of Highly Effective People: 30th Anniversary Edition"*, (Simon & Schuster, 2020) 109.

begin with the end in mind. Differing paths to the common objective no longer seemed like battles. We were on the same team working toward the same outcome. When we focus on our goals and our objective, it can help the conversations flow in less combative, more collaborative, productive, sustainable, win - win directions.

Possible objectives of a caregiving journey might be:

- Honor your family member's wishes to age in place for as long as possible while helping them maintain their independence and dignity.
- Prioritize health and well-being of both caregiver and family member receiving care.
- Find happiness in the present moment so that you maximize memories and minimize regret.

Reflect

- Think of the last conflict with your care recipient. Did winning this battle help you achieve your objectives, or did it derail your momentum toward your objectives?
- What might you have done differently to achieve a win - win outcome?

Journal

- Write out your objectives for your caregiving journey.

- In what ways might you be wrestling for control? What would happen if you shed the battle armor?
- Envision how it would be to no longer feel stress over the battles? Write a few thoughts in your journal.

Practice

- The next time a conflict arises, take a minute before responding. Think about your journey objectives. Think about the significance of this conflict in the scope of the journey.

When Losing is Winning

One reason that caregiving is stressful is due to obstacles. Obstacles make us emotional, and emotion clouds our thinking and our clear view of the obstacle. Emotions magnify the obstacle's power and, in doing so, can minimize our power. Acceptance can help us flip the obstacle so that it works for us rather than against us. When we acknowledge that a situation is not ideal but move to acceptance, we can then make choices that allow us to turn an obstacle into an opportunity. Reframing allows us to move from a position of perceived losing to winning.

We encounter many obstacles while caregiving. Our care recipient may feel like an obstacle at times. Other examples include the healthcare system, community systems and family dynamics. When we ask ourselves how we might use this situation to our advantage, we can examine it with a different lens. With this strategy, we can take back our power and see the gifts that the obstacles obscure, the gifts that are hiding in plain sight.

For example, maybe you loved to travel, and caregiving responsibilities curtailed your ability to be away from your home for any length of time. How could you use that time to your advantage? You might study the language and culture of your favorite or next destination. You could collect your memories and photos and write a travel memoir. Creating a detailed plan to see all the places on your bucket list when caregiving responsibilities come to an end is another option.

What if you flipped the script from "I have to be a caregiver" to "I get to be a caregiver"? What might your caregiving journey reveal? With training, practice, and a disciplined perspective, we can begin to look at challenges differently and see the opportunity more quickly. We may even bypass the negative emotions altogether. When we see a clear path forward, we avoid the negative feelings from uncertainty and the painful emotions from negative thoughts. We will not likely begin to welcome obstacles, but they will no longer paralyze us.

The first step in script flipping is awareness of the obstacle and the negative thought. Then lean into the negative thoughts around the obstacle by identifying precisely what is frustrating about the situation. Explore the uncomfortable feelings. What are the emotions you are experiencing, and what is causing them? Then look at the problem from the perspectives of all involved. What might be each person's challenges? Assess the validity of your own thoughts. Is there something you might be missing in your interpretation of events? Once you have a clearer idea of the situation from all angles, center yourself with a few deep breaths. What is a potential gift looming under the obstacle? What positive outcome might be revealed? Imagine yourself managing the situation with confidence. What will it take to get to that more empowered place? What is the first step you can take to creating the new reality?

A new perspective will not make caregiving easier. However, aspects of caregiving will be easier to accept when you discover the gift beneath the obstacle and use it as an opportunity for growth or discovery. Regular practice will cultivate emotional resilience. We learn to "struggle well" and shift quickly from perceived challenge to "what's next?". Soon you will progress through the steps so fast that the path from obstacle to empowerment will require little thought. You will flow with the current and move freely through and around obstacles.

Another strategy to help you flow in the direction of the current is to incorporate positive self-talk in the form of a mantra. An empowering phrase can help us reframe our thoughts. The practice of repeating a mantra during good times and bad can help us stay in flip-the-script mode.

Here are a few possibilities:

- I am enough.
- I am present.
- I am on the right path.
- Freedom comes from within. I am free.
- I choose kindness.
- I am learning. I am growing.

Reflect

- Think of a time in your life when you faced an enormous obstacle and were able to use it as a springboard to a better situation. Can you remember feeling the shift in your motivation? The resilience that you demonstrated is your power.
- What obstacles have you faced while caring for your family member? Think of one obstacle. How does the obstacle make you feel? Sit with those feelings for a few minutes.
- Begin to shift your perspective. What opportunity might you be missing due to the focus on your feelings?

Journal

- Describe a recent or current obstacle. What happened? What emotions did the obstacle evoke? How did you feel when facing the obstacle?

- What about that obstacle presented the most significant challenge?
- What would the obstacle look like if you flipped the obstacle over and examined it from all angles?
- What steps will allow you to transform the obstacle into an opportunity?
- What are the possible gifts that have been obscured by the obstacle?

Practice

- Begin the steps you identified in your journal to enable you to turn the obstacle into an opportunity.

2 SET, MODIFY & MAINTAIN BOUNDARIES: RESPECT THE RIVERBANK

Compassionate people ask for what they need. They say no when they need to, and when they say yes, they mean it. They're compassionate because their boundaries keep them out of resentment.

BRENÉ BROWN,
RISING STRONG

CARING FOR DAD changed our roles and responsibilities and, therefore, our relationship, which shifted from parent and adult child to care recipient and caregiver. As obligations changed, it was essential to reevaluate roles, relationships, and limits so that I, along with fellow caregivers helping me with Dad, felt respected and supported. Evaluating and setting boundaries was a process that continued to evolve throughout the experience. I learned that when I felt anger, it was often time to add, reinforce, or modify a boundary. Once signaled, awareness helped me determine if the anger was due to a crossed or missing boundary.

Boundaries are critical because they protect us from burnout. With that in mind, the best time to set boundaries is when you are wading into caregiving. You may have started helping with finances or running errands. Tasks that are at first occasionally added will increase and become the priorities in your days and weeks. Without boundaries, it is easy to place our well-being last. When this happens, our emotional state and our coping abilities are diminished, leading to feelings of overwhelm, burnout, and a state of being that is not sustainable.

In addition to relationships changing with our care recipient, relationships change with other family members and friends. Boundaries can help determine who is on your care team and who is only adding drama to the experience. You will find yourself in the new role of communicating and coordinating care for your family member, and it can feel awkward and intimidating. Boundaries will help you manage professional interactions with people who are helping with an intimate situation.

In the beginning, I started by helping Dad a few days a week. It wasn't my conscious intention, but two days a week turned into assisting with daily activities. Bit by bit, we can begin to give up our hobbies and interests until we are entrenched without a clear way out from under the tasks. What starts as fulfilling work becomes oppressive and frustrating when we don't keep our life. Keeping our life means protecting our other relationships and protecting ourselves from burnout. In this way, boundaries are a form of self-care. Self-imposed boundaries may be the most valuable. We can set a boundary around worry and when we realize that our anxiety is not productive, it may be time to move to acceptance.

An opportunity to set boundaries arose with a caregiver who happened to be a neighbor. When my husband and I moved out of Dad's place, we paid a neighbor, Mary, to check on him daily. Her visits were incredibly comforting when we were out of town. If I could not reach Dad, Mary and I could communicate via email or phone. She and Dad would visit for an hour each day. She often brought food. It was the perfect arrangement until Joe and I moved back in. We had told anyone who visited Dad regularly to just walk in the door because he was frequently in the back painting or watching tv and would not hear the bell or be able to get to the door quickly. Mary had become used to entering Dad's home, tidying up, and helping wherever she saw a need. This arrangement no longer worked when we moved back into his home. Her visits - up to three times a day - were disruptive. I learned that Dad did not appreciate the doting attention and would have preferred her visits be limited to three times a week rather than every day. Also, he did not need nor want any additional food, so the extra food was another source of frustration for him.

I knew it was time to have a conversation with Mary, and I carefully planned what I wanted to share with her. I realized my culpability in creating this situation and wanted to convey how grateful we were for all that she had been doing for Dad and us. The circumstances had changed, and it was necessary to make some changes to our arrangements. We agreed on a specific time that she would visit, once a day, and I thanked her for the food she had been bringing but asked that she not continue. She agreed to these requests. I was asking her to do less and was going to continue to pay her the same rate. Mary honored the new guidelines for one full day. After that, the food kept coming, and she would pop in several times a day. I sent the food back with her and reinforced the time of day upon which we had agreed. I made several more failed attempts at setting and reinforcing boundaries with Mary, and finally had to end the working relationship altogether. It took a few more conversations to get back to neighborly relations that respected privacy.

The boundary challenges did not end completely, but with the lessons learned, I understood my role in the relationship and communicated and reinforced boundaries with intention and compassion. I began to look at setting boundaries as a way to show respect: for Dad's wishes, for Joe's, for mine, and for anyone helping us care for Dad. If boundaries were not set and reinforced early, the result was anger, hurt, and resentment all around. I began to set boundaries to protect our time, our emotions, our energy, my capacity for compassion, and our values. When boundaries enabled us to interact according to our values, including respect and collaboration, everything flowed much smoother, there were fewer conflicts, less resentment, and we were navigating the caregiving experience sustainably.

I learned a bit too late that boundaries prevent burnout and that healthy boundaries help us maintain healthy relationships. Caregiver burnout occurs when we have given too much of ourselves. Establishing boundaries is a way to communicate our needs. Maintaining boundaries provides the opportunity to be more in control of our time and how we spend it. Without boundaries, the overwhelm of caregiving felt like being on the river without a paddle, bouncing from bank to bank with little control. Setting boundaries enabled me to direct the care team in a way that kept us all heading generally in the same direction, working together with the flow. Setting boundaries was a form of self-respect, and I realized that when I chose when to give, I saved enough of myself so that I was able to give when I chose.

Several barriers make setting boundaries hard. One common barrier is that because we have not been taught how to set boundaries, we don't recognize the need. Another barrier occurs when we realize a boundary is necessary but feel guilty about setting the boundary. Also, because boundaries we've tried to set might have been rejected or resisted, we become hesitant to try again. We may be told that we are selfish for setting the boundary, leading to guilt and confusion about the boundary's validity. We may be interacting with someone who does not set their own boundaries or respect those set by others. In this case, consistent reinforcement may be challenging due to uncomfortable confrontations. These uncomfortable confrontations may cause us to ignore a crossed boundary.

While setting boundaries can feel selfish, the opposite is true. Well maintained boundaries are a gift to you and those in your caregiving circle. The confidence to stand firm will come from being clear in your intention and from your communication. Practice will make the process easier. When you start to feel guilty about setting the boundary, remind yourself that setting boundaries is not selfish but an essential part of self-care as a caregiver. Boundaries will allow you to sustain yourself as you provide care. They will protect your compassion reserves so that you can provide the care that is in line with your values.

How we communicate boundaries is important. Here are a few tips for effective communication that have proven to be effective in my caregiving journey:

- Be clear on your intention so that you can be clear in your communication.
- Respectfully and with as few words as possible, communicate your boundary.
- Word the request in terms of what you need and why you need it rather than using the word "you." For example, "I need some space…" rather than, "You need to stop…".
- Explain the consequences if the boundary is crossed.
- Be firm and unapologetic.

If we are comfortable saying "no" and accepting a "no" from others, we understand and respect healthy boundaries. It may be that you are skilled at setting healthy boundaries at work but are less confident setting boundaries with family and friends. Learning to establish and maintain boundaries in a new setting takes awareness and practice. With practice, we can determine when boundaries are too rigid, too flexible, or just right. For example, there are varying degrees of "opening up" to people and sharing personal information. The extreme ends of sharing are "rarely opening up" vs. "oversharing." Somewhere in the middle is where healthy boundaries are formed. Another example of too rigid vs. too flexible is never asking for help vs. never saying no to a request for help. A boundary that is just right will help us not become overly independent or too detached.

Boundaries may be set with your care recipient, those who help you care for your care recipient, or anyone who impacts the care you provide for your care recipient. Personal boundaries are complicated because you can't see them, and they may need to change with circumstances. Healthy boundaries will help relationships feel supportive rather than strained under the stress of caregiving. Boundaries will help prevent resentment that can result when we give up too much of our life to caregiving, or a well-meaning person offers unwelcome advice or attempts to help in a way that is not helpful.

Defining a limit around care responsibilities is one of the most critical boundaries we can set to minimize resentment. Caregiving tasks can quickly shift from manageable to overwhelming. Determine how much time and effort you can spend on helping your family member and have a plan ready to get help when the limit has been reached.

Another limit may be necessary when care responsibilities involve physical risk or become too intimate for your comfort. For example, you may decide that you will not be able to help your family member with showering or toileting. Challenges may develop from living in the same space. Relationship dynamics may be exposed that would otherwise have been kept private. For example, your family member may be privy to uncomfortable conversations between you and your young children or between you and your spouse. Boundaries can help us share appropriate personal information without oversharing relationship details or receiving unwarranted opinions. Shared space also keeps us in a heightened state of awareness regarding our care recipient's mood. We can't be responsible for someone else's happiness or contentment. If we find that our care recipient's mood dictates our mood, it is a signal to revisit boundaries.

Consequences are crucial to proper boundary settings, and this can be complicated when dealing with an aging adult with cognitive decline or a dementia diagnosis. If your care recipient cannot remember that a boundary was set, then the rules must be self-enforced. For example, if you have requested that a parent does not enter your room without knocking, but this continues to occur because your care recipient forgets, you will need to lock the door.

Setting boundaries with paid caregivers and aides is essential. Limits can be set around sharing personal information. The folks who help you care for your family member can become like a part of the family. If this relationship becomes too familiar, it can be uncomfortable communicating when there is a concern with how tasks are accomplished or if personal conversation interferes with responsibilities. Another way in which limits may be set is around light housekeeping. If you share space with your care recipient, you may appreciate that the aide helps keep your family member's living spaces clean but prefer to manage your personal areas yourself. Clear communication can avoid hurt feelings when a kind gesture from your aide feels like an unwelcome invasion. In general, when more rigid boundaries are established early, it is easier to move to more flexible boundaries. It is not easy, however, to start with flexible boundaries and shift to more rigid boundaries.

Boundaries with family members can help us maintain relationships. Limits may be set around when to have conversations regarding your loved one's care. Suppose a family member frequently drops by and offers suggestions and advice. In that case, it may feel like criticism when you are exhausted and overwhelmed by the responsibilities of day-to-day care. It may help to establish guidelines around communication concerning care. With mindfulness and compassion, you can let them know that they are important to you and that the topic is important, but that in the moment, you cannot give it the attention that is deserved. An informal meeting once a week could be more productive. Another time when setting boundaries is important but can feel uncomfortable is when your care recipient is transitioning. Well-meaning family members may insist that you take a break, but maybe you don't want to do so, or you would rather take a short break. This is for you to decide.

Boundaries with friends become important as caregiving intensifies. Friends of your care recipient may drop in unannounced, and it might disrupt the schedule. The disruption might start a stress snowball. Social interaction is important. Communication and coordination with them will show respect for the relationship and demonstrate that you value the friendship. Setting boundaries around visits will ensure that quality time is spent between your care recipient and visitor and that things don't go off the rails as soon as they leave.

Boundaries with neighbors may be needed due to similar circumstances as with friends and family. As care needs intensify, the previously welcomed drop-in visit may start to feel like an imposition. It may be that a neighbor is offering interfering advice that is causing friction between you and your family member. Establishing boundaries around visits and communication can help preserve relationships and allow mutually beneficial interactions.

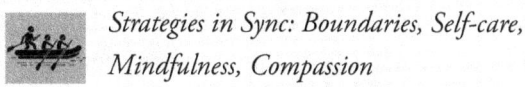

Strategies in Sync: Boundaries, Self-care, Mindfulness, Compassion

Here are a few examples of how self-care can work together with other strategies and boundaries to create a more sustainable caregiving experience.

- Self-care: Boundaries help us prioritize and protect self-care when we schedule self-care activities and communicate that we are engaged in an activity that supports our well-being. Without boundaries, if our scheduled self-care is compromised, we may feel anger.
- Mindfulness: The awareness that we cultivate through mindfulness helps us pause and identify that the source of the anger is a crossed boundary. Then, we can reinforce the boundary with compassion.
- Compassion: We feel and show compassion because we have created a habit of prioritizing our well-being and maintain replenished compassion reserves.

Reflect

- How has the relationship changed between you and your care recipient? Have boundaries changed to reflect the new relationship?
- Consider this quote from Jessica Moore, "Anger is a sentry, stalking the edges of our boundaries

and standing ready to defend them."[7] Think of a recent or memorable time when you felt anger. Was the anger due to a crossed boundary?

Journal

- List the people who are a regular part of your care team.
- What opportunities exist to establish, adjust, or reinforce a boundary?
- Describe the conversation that would allow you to set or reinforce the boundary with compassion.

Practice

- Be mindful of feelings of anger so that you recognize when a boundary has been crossed.
- Journal the steps that will allow you to establish, adjust, or reinforce a crossed boundary with one of the people on your care team.
- Begin the conversation with that person. It might take more than one.

---

7   Jessica Moore, Goodreads.com, *https://www.goodreads.com/quotes/9400928-anger-is-a-sentry-stalking-the-edges-of-our-boundaries*, accessed June 2, 2020

3 CULTIVATE AWARENESS THROUGH MINDFULNESS: FLOW FROM THE PRESENT MOMENT

Stress is caused by being here but wanting to be there or being in the present, but wanting to be in the future. It's a split that tears you apart inside.

ECKHART TOLLE,
THE POWER OF NOW

WE HAVE MORE than 6,000 thoughts in a single day![8] How many of those 6,000 thoughts do you imagine are positive? Negative? Repetitive? Mindfulness is a tool that allows us to gain control over worries through the practice of being in a state of consciousness where we are present and aware of our thoughts, body, and emotions.

---

8 Julie Tseng and Jordan Poppenk, "Brain meta-state transitions demarcate thoughts across task contexts exposing the mental noise of trait neuroticism," *Nat Commun* 11, 3480 (2020), *https://doi.org/10.1038/s41467-020-17255-9*

When we are present and focused on the task at hand, our mind is not wandering, and we are not ruminating about the past or anxious about the future. We can use this hyper-sensitive state of awareness to recognize when we shift from a focus on the present to a past or future worry. Awareness through mindfulness helps us bring the worries to the surface and into the light, where we can see how they hold us hostage and have power over our actions. When you have this new perspective and observe the thought that caused the worry, the connection to the emotion is broken. You may question the thought and disagree with it before it results in a reaction or an emotion. You take back the power and develop the inner strength and calm that comes from having control over your mind. You are able to cultivate a calm and even-tempered mind.

Caring for a family member involves numerous tasks and responsibilities that can become overwhelming. We may be in the middle of accomplishing one job, and our mind is on the many other items that we need to get done. With work that revolves around family, emotions are at the center of every decision, event, and experience. Our family member's physical and mental abilities are often declining, and their personalities may change as well. Negative emotions, heightened by worry about our family member and the future, take a toll on our well-being and our ability to manage care. When we are under emotional stress, we think less clearly, our sleep suffers, and often our support systems are no longer available in part because we are no longer available.

The more we practice mindfulness, the more skilled we become at being present and aware of our mind's inner workings and how to break harmful habits such as dwelling on past mistakes or future worries. We can practice mindfulness throughout the day as well as in meditation sessions. Mindfulness practice teaches our brain to disconnect from the worry cycle. When we are present and aware, we are not anxious about the upcoming section of swift water in our caregiver river or obsessing over how we could have better navigated the last obstacle that blocked our path. With mindfulness, we live in the moment and navigate our experience with control of our thoughts and actions. With mindfulness, we use awareness and perception to quickly adjust and readjust as the obstacles appear.

The consistent practice of mindfulness will help us cultivate awareness of our surroundings and our internal environment. It can feel like time slows down and allows us to assess and respond with measured thoughts, words, and actions. Another state of consciousness that results from being present is flow. When we are in a state of flow, it can feel like time speeds up. Hours can feel like minutes when we are so focused on the task at hand that we are entirely unaware of our surroundings because our awareness is solely on our activity. We are fully present and move through the actions with intuition, without thought or concern about the next step. In this state of consciousness, we flow with rather than against the current. All drama drifts away, and we intuitively navigate obstacles. We let go and accept the flow that is streaming directly from the present moment. When we are in a state of flow, we resist nothing because there is nothing to resist. The result is freeing acceptance. All is as it should be. What activities lead you into a flow state? The activities may involve creating art, music, or writing. Flow activities may be tied to a form of exercise such as running or yoga. Some may find flow in folding laundry or cleaning. When you incorporate these activities into your day, you are practicing mindfulness, cultivating awareness, and releasing stress as the thoughts that cause negative emotions are released.

During the first few years of caregiving, I felt utterly controlled by emotions. My internal and external responses felt automatic as if I didn't have command over my reactions. I reacted inwardly and outwardly to Dad's behaviors and opinions. I reacted when healthcare professionals were insensitive, or healthcare systems created rather than alleviated stress. I reacted when aides added to my workload rather than reduced it. I held in my frustrations and anger until I vented later to my husband, which was okay in small doses but not healthy when the frustrations felt insurmountable. I used the unjust situation as justification for decisions that were not in my best interest. I ruminated, and instead of choosing a self-care activity or taking a break, I made less healthy choices, which added to feelings of being out of control in a downward spiral.

I was confused by my inability to remain calm and disciplined as I had when I faced stressful encounters at work. Why were my skills not serving me well in my new role as Dad's caregiver? Research led me to the concepts of mindfulness, stillness, and being present as a better way to manage my thoughts and, in turn, control my emotions and reactions. Practicing meditation was promoted as a way to achieve a calmer, more thoughtful state of being. I had tried meditation off and on over the years and had failed to quiet racing thoughts. It was too hard. I abandoned each attempt. This time, I had unprecedented motivation and the assistance of technology. The apps I found featured guided meditations, meditation music, and sleep stories. In my earlier attempts, I still failed to focus on nothingness. The worries entered any open space I created. This time, however, I didn't give up.

Meditation became more comfortable, and I looked forward to meditating. Then, I noticed that I could mentally pause and analyze a situation, including my response as it was unfolding. I was both a participant and a spectator. In real-time, I connected my evolving thoughts to their resulting emotions. Meditation was the primary method I used to cultivate mindfulness. Practicing meditation and mindfulness trained me to pause my racing thoughts and use that space for awareness and intuition. As a result, I was more empowered and in control. I was less stressed. I managed the caregiving journey more sustainably, no longer controlled by the swirl of negative emotions that kept me focused on problems, rather than solutions.

As I cultivated mindfulness, I gained awareness of how and where my body tensed when I felt stress. This awareness helped me recognize when I was consumed by a worry rather than focusing on the present. With clarity, came calm and compassion for myself and others. When potential problems loomed, I mindfully shifted to solution mode, bypassing the stress that came from fear of the outcome.

Awareness, through mindfulness, gives us several opportunities to pause the story and rewrite it. When we act rather than react, we control our emotions; we are fully aware of the forces at play and act with intention. Acting with intent also reduces regret. Reaction and regret fuel guilt and resentment, which are emotions that wear us down and lead to burnout, an unsustainable state.

Mindful listening is a natural extension of being more present. Being present and aware helped me tune into the shift in my emotions in real time and recognize when my feelings prevented me from being open to hearing or understanding the resistance to reaching an agreement or resistance to acceptance. With presence and awareness, I could assess what information I needed to better understand the disagreement and ask thoughtful questions to gain clarity. In the process, Dad felt heard. I made an effort to listen with openness rather than with motives to craft a counterargument. I looked for signs that my ego was sabotaging a possible resolution.

As I employed a more mindful approach and became more aware of potential problems and conflicts, I thought of Ben and Roz Zander, the authors of The Art of Possibility: Transforming Professional and Personal Life.[9] In their book, Ben shares a strategy that can help us experience the power of the pause. Between that moment of incident and reaction, observe and say to yourself, "How fascinating." It offers an opportunity not to take ourselves so seriously. It gives us a moment to get out of our head and get over ourselves. We can observe a situation and watch it unfold with curiosity and maybe even see the humor in the circumstances. When Dad said or did something that caused an emotional or physical reaction, I learned to pause and wonder more about my reaction and his motivations. I took time to explore beneath the surface and ask questions to understand better what I was missing. I began to read the river and flow smoothly around the obstacles rather than react to them instinctively and without reflection, upsetting the smooth progress.

Cultivating mindfulness also allowed me to reconnect to the skills that I had used effectively in situations outside of caregiving. The self-reliance that I developed due to feeling more empowered and in control minimized

---

[9] Roseamund Stone Zander and Benjamin Zander, *"The Art of Possibility: Transforming Professional and Personal Life"*, (Penguin Books, 2002)

the feelings of isolation and loneliness in the caregiving role. With continued practice, I saw improvement. I was less stressed. I began to believe that I would survive, and that hope helped me move from surviving to thriving in my role caring for Dad. The work was still difficult, but it was sustainable.

In summary, the benefits are many when we are present and aware:

- Our responses become less impulsive and less reactive when we observe our thoughts and emotions without letting ourselves get immersed in them.
- Using expanded self-awareness and awareness of the present moment, we can reserve judgment and accept an experience with curiosity, openness, and, ultimately, clarity.
- Enhanced self-reflection and self-observation develops and strengthens our coping skills and resilience.
- When we focus on the present, the stress associated with ruminating on the past or future is minimized. We can better concentrate on managing the immediate challenges and, with clarity, find solutions.

Meditation is one way to practice mindfulness and it can take many forms, including guided meditations, walking meditation, visualization, reflection, or sound bath meditation. All forms of meditation have one aspect in common: sustaining attention on one thing for an extended period to achieve a state of consciousness where your mind is clear and relaxed. Meditation allows us to see and explore the cause of our emotions. With this insight, we can manage those feelings and emotions. Studies have connected meditation practice to improved sleep, lower blood pressure, reduced reactions, decreased anxiety and stress, enhanced clarity and problem-solving ability.[10] These are all integral to sustainability while in the caregiving role. Meditation has been shown to improve empathy and increase compassion, resulting in improved relationships.[11]

A traditional form of meditating is merely sitting with a straight posture and calming your mind. A typical meditation form is mindful meditation, anchoring attention on the breath, doing a body scan, or silently repeating a mantra. You can start with as little as a two-minute session and increase the duration when it feels comfortable. Work up to ten-minute sessions. Micro-dosing meditation has proven benefits to stress relief, clarity, and decision making. Consistency is critical, so daily practice is essential. You may want to meditate at the same time each day. Protect your practice with a routine and

---

10   "8 Things to Know About Meditation for Health," *NIH National Center for Complimentary and Integrative Health*, *https://www.nccih. nih.gov/health/tips/things-to-know-about-meditation-for-health*, accessed November 13, 2021

11   Jennifer l. Goetz, Dacher Keltner, and Emiliana Simon-Thomas, "Compassion: an evolutionary analysis and empirical review," *Psychological bulletin*, 136, no. 3 (2010): 351–374. https://doi.org/10.1037/a0018807

boundaries. Apps such as Headspace, Calm, and Chopra are useful tools to motivate and help develop abilities.

Walking meditation is an active, mindful form of meditating that lets us connect the mind and body to the rhythm of walking. You may prefer to try this form of meditation first in familiar surroundings where you will be comfortable getting used to the practice. Before you begin, you will want to spend 30 seconds centering or grounding yourself to feel the connection to your body. Standing still, take a few deep breaths and feel the ground under your feet. As you bring awareness to your body, scan from top to bottom and note any sensations. The principle is to pay attention to each step. You might count your steps and connect your breath to your steps so that your pace remains slow and steady. You may also connect to the five senses and note what you see, smell, hear, feel, or taste. You might say a word or mantra on the inhale and exhale. Because your destination is the present moment, the pace will be much slower than a walk for exercise. Repeat the 30 seconds of grounding at the end of the meditation.

When you find what types of meditation resonate with you, you might mix them up and use what works best based on your mood or stress level. A meditation coach once said that there is no correct or incorrect way to meditate, just better ways to meditate. Remove the pressure to be perfect and experiment with the many ways to disengage from the constant stream of thoughts that cause stress.

Yoga is another activity that helps cultivate awareness through mindfulness. The core purpose of yoga is to quiet the thoughts that prevent our mind from resting at its natural, peaceful state. During practice, attention is placed on the breath as you move through yoga poses (asanas). A simple five-minute yoga flow that includes breathing exercises (pranayama) can calm the body and mind and release anxiety. Practicing yoga before meditation will promote a more profound mindfulness experience.

We can also improve our ability to shift to the present moment by practicing breathing exercises. A simple exercise that can help you feel calmer is to count to five on the inhale, hold for a count of five, and exhale while counting to five. Repeated several times, this practice can work as well as a lullaby when you wake up in the middle of the night, and the worries lurk like shadows in the dark. There are many different breathing exercises, and it is helpful to have a few memorized and have handy when caught off guard by stress.

Since cultivating mindfulness takes practice and consistency, it is helpful to practice by weaving mindful acts into everyday life. Throughout the day, there are opportunities to refocus our attention on the present moment and be fully present in our life. We can immerse ourselves in the flow of daily experiences such as cooking or washing our hands. Practicing during less stressful activities will help you develop the ability to remain present through the more challenging situations. Here are a few ways to incorporate mindfulness into your day to reduce anxiety and stress:

- In line at the checkout counter – Take a deep breath and hold it for 5 seconds. Release the breath slowly. Do this a few times and feel the tension release from your body.
- Anywhere – Silently, name all of the things or colors that you can see.
- At a traffic light – Keep a stone or small rock within reach and hold it at a red light, run your fingers over it. Alternatively, notice the feel of the steering wheel, the texture, the temperature. Is the seat firm or soft? Bring your attention to the physical.
- Looking out the window – What do you see? Look at each object as if you were seeing it for the first time. Notice the shapes, colors, movement. Practice increasing awareness without fixating on any one object.
- Eating – Notice the appearance of the texture, how it feels in your hand or on your tongue. Note the flavor and how different flavors interact with each other to create layers of flavor.
- Transitions between activities – Take the seconds between putting down your phone and picking up your coffee cup to bring awareness to the moment.

- Altercation – Be curious. It isn't possible to be angry and interested at the same time. Become curious as to why your care recipient is acting in a certain way. Instead of reacting, ask them.

When we develop this strategy and skill of being present and aware, we will have undoubtedly changed while on the caregiving journey. We can carry our new superpower into the future, which is now.

Strategies in Sync: Mindfulness, Boundaries, Self-care, Compassion

Awareness helps us hone the strategies and identify how they connect and fit our situation to best support our well-being.

- Boundaries and Routines: We can incorporate mindfulness practices into routines and prioritize and set boundaries around the routines to safeguard the activities.
- Self-care: Mindfulness practices calm our mind and body and are a self-care activity that also trains our minds and bodies to seek this state of calm.
- Compassion: When we are mindful of the present moment, we respond in accordance with our values.

Reflect

- How does this quote resonate with you regarding caregiving? "Most humans are never fully present in the now because unconsciously they believe that the next moment must be more important than this one. But then you miss your whole life, which is never not now." Eckhart Tolle[12]
- Do you agree with this statement: "Our power is in the present"? How can it apply to your current caregiving journey?

Journal

- Which mindfulness practices appeal to you?
- How can mindfulness and boundaries work together to create a less stressful caregiving experience for you?

Practice

- Fritz Perls has been credited with saying, "Lose your mind and come to your senses."[13] Use the five senses to refocus attention on your surroundings. This is particularly powerful when combined with time in nature.

---

12 Tolle, Eckhart (@EckhartTolle). Twitter Post, May 28, 2021. 6:40pm, https://twitter.com/eckharttolle/status/1398423842729590789?lang=en

13 Frederick Salomon Perls. AZQuotes.com, Wind and Fly LTD, 2021. https://www.azquotes.com/quote/421181, accessed November 11, 2021.

- Incorporate one mindfulness practice a day. It may be a 10-minute meditation, using curiosity to pause the moment, a breathing exercise to calm the nerves, or another strategy that allows you to experience stillness.
- As negative thoughts enter your mind during meditation or throughout the day, label them. You might choose the label fear, ego, grudge, regret, worry, and then let the thought go.
- When your mind wanders, bring your focus back to the present by taking a few deep breaths. You can also focus for a moment on your heart to center yourself in the present moment.

4 REIMAGINE SELF-CARE: EXPEDITIONS REQUIRE STAMINA

I have become clear about at least one thing: self-care is never a selfish act — it is simply good stewardship of the only gift I have, the gift I was put on earth to offer to others.

PARKER J. PALMER,

LET YOUR LIFE SPEAK

CARING FOR A family member requires stamina. Caregiving takes both emotional and physical tolls, and these consequences are connected. When we struggle emotionally, our body suffers. We could experience gastrointestinal troubles, aches and pains caused by stress or unhealthy weight changes. Our emotional state is compromised when our bodies are in distress due to lack of sleep or inadequate nutrition. When we are unwell physically, we struggle to think clearly and find it difficult to achieve a state of balance and calm. The relationship between our physical well-being and our emotional well-being is why it is crucial to participate in self-care activities that protect and preserve the mind, body, and mind-body connection to prevent burnout. When we focus on all aspects of our well-being, we can perform at our best while navigating an intense caregiving expedition.

You may not have recognized your hobbies and interests as self-care before caregiving. Going to the gym, reading for pleasure, sleeping, or spending time with friends was just a part of life. As we begin to care for a family member and priorities shift, it is not uncommon to give up our interests and hobbies bit by bit until our entire life revolves around caregiving. The activities that we enjoy, the ones that renew our energy, and that help us feel connected to what makes us feel whole, are each a version of self-care. The challenge for you as a caregiver is to continue to modify and experience what brings you joy when layers of responsibilities and stress become a part of your day. You can discover new caregiver-friendly interests that help you reset and care for yourself as you care for your family member. Therefore, self-care will look different for each person and may change from day to day, possibly minute to minute.

Reimagining self-care can include:

- Identifying the activities that support our well-being and fit within our ever-evolving situation

- Prioritizing the activities by scheduling them or incorporating them into routines
- Protecting the activities and routines with boundaries

As the caregiving experience intensifies, self-care opportunities may come in minutes rather than hours. We can make the most of those minutes by redefining self-care as often as necessary to fit within our day, within our routines. You might create a go-to list of restorative activities to have several options to choose from depending on your mood, needs, available time, and space.

What reimagined self-care looks like:

Self-care prior to caregiving	Self-care during caregiving
Yoga: 1-hour yoga class 3 times per week at your local fitness club	**Yoga:** 5-15 minutes of yoga poses each day during your scheduled self-care break in your designated comfy corner in your family member's home
Time with friends: Weekly get together for drinks and dinner to catch up on the latest news and gossip	**Time with friends:** Bi-monthly coffee to stay connected and hear the latest news and gossip or a walk outdoors while talking with a friend on the phone
Travel: A getaway to a distant location	**Travel:** 5-15 minutes learning a new language, culture, or cuisine so that when you are able to travel, your experience will be enhanced, and you stay connected to the joys of travel
Tennis: Participation on a team and travel to tournaments	**Tennis:** Meet a friend a couple of times a month for a game
Music: Attend a concert or music festival	**Music:** Have a calming playlist at the ready

Two Categories of Self-care

It is helpful to consider two primary categories of self-care. The first category, essential well-being self-care, is the foundation of our physical, mental, and emotional health and is often neglected when the caregiving experience is new and intense. Essential well-being could be considered maintenance. Schedule the wellness visit, the dentist appointment, and other appointments that may have been neglected because you have had to place your health priorities behind your care recipient's needs. Essential well-being includes getting an adequate quality and quantity of sleep, healthy nutrition and hydration, and exercise or some form of movement. These components are necessary to maintain the energy required when we are caring for a family member. The second category includes our pursuits beyond the essential self-care elements, the more varied and value-added activities that calm our minds and reenergize our bodies.

Essential well-being self-care

Taking care of our basic well-being requirements can seem impossible when we suddenly drop into an intense caregiving experience or have arrived without preparation. We are merely trying to survive. Sleep, exercise, and nutrition, including hydration, warrant special attention because when in balance, we feel better, and we perform more optimally.

Sleep

Good quality sleep is crucial for us to be at our best when facing the challenges of caregiving. Lack of proper sleep affects our ability to think clearly, and causes us to feel disorganized, be quicker to anger, and feel hopeless. Sufficient sleep has been linked to benefits such as heart health, a more robust immune system, better brain function, improved mood, and reduced stress.[14] Specifically, when we sleep well, our thinking is more precise, we are less susceptible to mental and physical illnesses, and we can better tolerate incidents that cause frustration.

But, while caring for a family member, our sleep quantity and quality can suffer due to care responsibilities, or we lie awake at night due to worries. If your care recipient is up at night and, as a result, you are up with them, you might consider having a nighttime aide to manage the period that would allow you to get a consistent night's sleep. Consistency is vital, so having a sleep routine and going to bed at the same time each evening enables our bodies to anticipate the time to wind down and prepare for rest. It is also helpful to be aware of our behaviors that contribute to healthy sleep and those that detract from a restful night's sleep.

It is recommended that we go to bed and get up each morning on a consistent schedule seven days a week. It is ideal to fall asleep within 15 to 20 minutes and sleep

---

14   Vicki Contie et al., "The Benefits of Slumber, Why You Need a Good Night's Sleep", *NIH News in Health* ISSN 1556-3898 (April 2013), https://newsinhealth.nih.gov/2013/04/benefits-slumber

between seven and nine hours. Since worries can wreak havoc and prevent us from falling asleep and keep us up during the early hours of the morning, the hour before bedtime is best spent engaged in calming activities such as reading, a nighttime meditation, or taking a warm bath. According to an article on the Popular Science website, "People who regularly take baths seem to have lower stress levels and be less depressed than people who just shower. Submerging yourself in water on the regular may even help make you less angry."[15] The simple acts of washing our face or brushing our teeth at the same time each night can trigger the body to prepare for sleep.

Drinking tea can be a helpful part of your evening ritual. Teas such as chamomile and passionflower contain apigenin, which has been connected to calming effects and reduced anxiety, helping us relax and fall asleep. It is recommended that we avoid eating within two hours of bedtime so that digestion is complete. Consuming caffeine and alcohol too late in the day is also counter to a good night's sleep.

Another way to set yourself up for a good night's sleep is to create a calm, serene, and dark sleeping space. Lavender, an essential oil that promotes calm, is often used in sprays or diffused to create a relaxing environment. Minimizing light, including light from phones and computers, is also recommended to support a full

---

15 Rachel Feltman, "To take the most relaxing bath ever, add some healthy tips", *Popular Science*, January 23, 2021, https://www.popsci.com/story/health/best-bath-tips-science/

night's sleep. You may consider using a dim nightlight in the bathroom to prevent the need to turn on a brighter light in the middle of the night. You could even start to dim the lights where you spend time an hour or two before bedtime.

An intentional review of the day can help avoid the random thoughts that keep us awake. You might include a practice of gratitude. Similarly, it may be helpful to write down the next day's activities and do any preparations that will enable you to feel more relaxed about what the next day holds.

Consider adding evening or bedtime mindfulness practices such as nighttime meditation practice or repeating a calming mantra. Breathing exercises, also known as the yoga practice, called pranayama, can help you fall asleep and help you get back to sleep when you wake up in the middle of the night and struggle to fall back asleep. Besides calming the mind and heart rate, specific breathing techniques such as box breathing, also known as samavritti, meaning equal breath, alter the blood's CO_2 mix, calming the body and mind, which will help us fall asleep.

Box breathing technique:
- Exhale completely while you count to four.
- Pause while you count to four.
- Inhale through your nose while you count to four.

- Pause and hold the breath while you count to four. Repeat steps 1 – 4.

Apps
Apps that offer sleep stories, music, meditations, the sounds of nature, or white noise designed to inspire sleep can be a significant aid to help you get to sleep or get back to sleep. A few apps to check out are, Calm, Headspace, Unplug Meditation, Wave Sleep, Unwind, Inscape, and White Noise. The Calm app has a sleep section of Sleep Stories that work as a lullaby and a section of Refreshing Nap Stories for ninja-level naps. Most apps have a trial period that will allow you to experiment and find what works best for you.

Experimenting with techniques and personalizing your ritual will help you dial in your formula for consistent, comfortable rest. Consider keeping a sleep diary to track what strategies and combinations work well. Keep track of your daytime energy levels to connect the efforts to positive results.

Exercise
Exercise can help us manage the stress that comes from the weighty responsibilities and worries surrounding caring for a family member. Movement has been connected to many physical and mental health benefits, including increased energy levels, improved mood, better sleep, and even increased feelings of confidence and con-

trol.[16] Any form of movement including exercise, yoga, dance, tai chi, paddling, and more can enhance mood. Exercise distracts us and shifts the tension in our bodies to a more relaxed state. Regular exercise has proven to offer long-term anxiety prevention benefits.[17] Choose whatever options bring you joy, add them to your routine, and protect the activity with boundaries.

Researchers in Britain discovered that even five minutes of exercise in nature can lift our mood. They call it "green exercise."[18] That means a quick walk around the block can help us reset. If you have more than five minutes, walking in nature offers multiple benefits, and you can make your steps even more meaningful with a few mindful practices. Here are some options to consider:

- Make mental notes of the nature you see. You might choose a theme and notice the trees along your path or pay particular attention to wildlife.
- Experience the walk using all your senses. What can you see, hear, smell, feel, and taste as you move through nature or your neighborhood?

---

16 Ashish Sharma, Vishal Madaan, and Frederick D. Petty, "Exercise for mental health." *Primary care companion to the Journal of clinical psychiatry*, 8(2) (2006): 106. https://doi.org/10.4088/pcc.v08n0208a

17 John J. Ratey, "Can exercise help treat anxiety?" *Harvard Health Publishing*, October 24, 2019, https://www.health.harvard.edu/blog/can-exercise-help-treat-anxiety-2019102418096

18 Jules N. Pretty, et al., "Green exercise in the UK countryside: Effects on health and psychological well-being, and implications for policy and planning." *Journal of Environmental Planning and Management*, 50 (2007), 211-231. 10.1080/09640560601156466.

- Focus on counting your breaths or your footsteps. This focus will help prevent the worries from creeping in and give you the peace that comes from the worry-free space. It is normal for worries to join you on your walk. Gently ask them to go away, so you may return to counting.

You could also combine a walk with other self-care activities such as connecting with a friend either in person or on the phone. You could listen to music, a podcast, or an audiobook. Another option is to work through a challenge that you are facing and take the opportunity to look at it from all perspectives to gain a better understanding and reframe the issues. Just the change in scenery can help us literally and figuratively have a new view.

There are also many videos and channels on YouTube that offer short, impactful micro workouts. There are subscription services that make a living room workout as effective as going to the gym.

One subscription service is Apple Fitness Plus. It offers a large selection of 10 and 20 minute workouts in categories such as yoga, high-intensity training (HIT), strength training, core, and dance that may all be done without equipment or with a few dumbbells of varying weights. There are several trainers and intensity options within each workout. New sessions are added regularly. An Apple watch is required, and the workouts can be viewed on an iPhone or with an Apple TV device. The subscription can be shared with up to six family members.

A less expensive option is a resistance band kit and YouTube videos. Vital Home Gym offers a typical kit. Therapy bands work well also and can be found on Amazon. Daily Burn and obé fitness are moderately priced membership services that offer streaming classes, including kickboxing, barre, yoga, dance, Pilates, and more. Yoga With Adriene, a YouTube channel with over 9 million subscribers, offers 700 videos that include mediations. She also has a Yoga with Adriene website. If you had or have a gym membership, there may be streaming classes as well. High-end Smart Home Gym Equipment options include Peloton, Mirror, and Tonal.

Nutrition
Nutrition plays a role in stress management. Choosing the foods that support our well-being can be challenging when managing care for a family member. It is helpful to understand which foods support our well-being, how they make a difference, and how to incorporate them into snacks and meals easily. It is important to eat regularly so that our brain is fueled and functioning at optimum levels to make difficult decisions. When we are hungry, we are more sensitive to the negative thoughts that drive negative emotions. We are also more likely to reach for food that may quell the hunger but will not be the best choice for health or to stimulate clear thinking. Foods high in sugar may give us an immediate energy boost but will ultimately cause our blood sugar and possibly mood to crash, resulting in increased feelings of stress. When we

are under stress, our bodies need more nutrients; fruits and vegetables are the best sources.[19] Also, stress weakens the immune system, making these nutrients even more crucial.

Current dietary guidelines may help as a starting point but should be tailored to meet your specific needs and preferences. The MyPlate Plan offered at MyPlate.gov could provide a starting point, or you may have a system for balanced eating that works for you. When you have determined your desired balance of protein, vegetables, fiber, and healthy fats, you can build your menu options.

Keys to success start with eating breakfast and eating at regularly scheduled intervals throughout the day, even if you aren't hungry. This way, when the unexpected task requires attention, hunger doesn't interfere. For the same reason, keep healthy snacks handy at home, in the car, a sack, or a purse that goes with you. Include nutrition in your routines and set boundaries so that you have healthy choices when priorities shift at the last minute.

The Verve: Body Mind and Health app is an example of the support available from technology to create and track plans for meals, exercise, and sleep. Verve is offered as a subscription service, a trending business model. It is vital to invest in your health and well-being early and

---

19   Adrian L Lopresti, "The Effects of Psychological and Environmental Stress on Micronutrient Concentrations in the Body: A Review of the Evidence." *Advances in nutrition*, 11(1) (2020): 103–112. https://doi.org/10.1093/advances/nmz082

consistently so that you stay strong throughout the caregiving experience.

Hydration

Simply staying well hydrated can reduce our stress levels. When our heart rate is elevated and breathing is more rapid, we lose fluid and are more likely to get dehydrated. When we are dehydrated, the levels of the stress hormone cortisol increase in our bodies. In addition, because our organs rely on water to function well, when we're dehydrated our body is stressed and not optimally supporting us.[20] This cycle can be disrupted by drinking more hydrating fluids. Calming herbal teas can hydrate and provide added stress-relieving benefits. Chamomile and mint teas are stress relievers, and tea-time is a self-care activity that will serve both the benefits of hydrating and pausing the day's stressors.

Restorative well-being self-care

In contrast to essential well-being self-care, there are other self-care activities that simply relieve stress. We have already explored mindfulness practices, breathing exercises and activities that get us moving.

Consider the following activities that you can re-imagine as self-care.

---

20 Barry M., Popkin, Kristen E. D'Anci, and Irwin H Rosenberg, "Water, hydration, and health." *Nutrition reviews*, 68(8) (2010): 439–458. https://doi.org/10.1111/j.1753-4887.2010.00304.x

Music

Create a "Reset my Mood" playlist. Research suggests that music can reduce stress and anxiety and improve cognitive brain function.[21] Because music affects both our mind and body, it is an excellent addition to self-care while caregiving.

Scents

Scents can bring peace. It is our previous experiences with odors that elicit a response. Certain smells will trigger specific memories and stimulate emotions based on those memories.[22] This learned response and connection to emotion can be used to your self-care advantage when you identify the odors that trigger calm and happy memories. Keep your happy scents handy.

Essential Oils

Oils from plant extracts support well-being in a variety of ways. You may want to experiment with oils as solutions for both you and your family member. There are many oils connected to reduced stress and improved mood.[23] A few to try include lavender, sandalwood, rose,

---

21   Myriam V. Thoma et al., "The effect of music on the human stress response", *PloS one*, **8, NO. 8 (2013),** https://doi.org/10.1371/journal.pone.0070156

22   *Sabrina Stierwalt*, "Why Do Smells Trigger Memories?" *Scientific American,* June 29, 2020, https://www.scientificamerican.com/article/why-do-smells-trigger-memories1/

23   Xiao Nan Lv, Zhu Jun Liu, Huan Jing Zhang and Chi Meng Tzeng, "Aromatherapy and the central nerve system (CNS): therapeutic

bergamot, chamomile, and jasmine. You might diffuse them in your comfy corner or carry a rollerball with you. Quality varies, so research and label reading are essential to ensure that the oil's effectiveness is not compromised or deficient.

Tea

Just like brushing our teeth can signal our mind and body that it is time for bed, the ritual of making tea can start to calm us as we prepare to take a break and relax. In addition, certain teas are credited with calming the nerves. Mint, chamomile, lavender, and rose are lauded as the best ingredients for a calming cup of tea. Find your favorite flavor. Check out Pukka's herbal teas: Revitalise with cinnamon, cardamom, ginger, or Love with chamomile, rose, and lavender.

Oasis

Create an oasis in your home where you can go to de-stress for a few minutes throughout the day. You might create a comfy, cozy corner within your care recipient's home so that you have a place to restore and regroup. Imagine surrounding yourself with LED candles, a calming scent, mood music, sounds of nature, tea, art, plant, or a tabletop Zen Garden and pillows in your favorite colors. You may add stones or other items that are comforting to hold.

---

mechanism and its associated genes," *Current drug targets*, 14, no. 8 (2013): 872–879. https://doi.org/10.2174/13894501113314080007

TV
Sometimes we need to escape or want to be entertained. You might take a break to watch a favorite show or have it on while cooking or doing chores.

Writing
Writing and the act of creating is excellent self-care when you can get lost in the process. Diary style, poems, or a gratitude journal are all good options. Look for a beautiful blank book to hold your unique thoughts. Have you wanted to write a novel? The caregiving years are a great time to start jotting down notes and then piecing them together. Take note of dialogue that comes to mind and begin to form the narrative.

Nature
If nature is your happy place, make spending time outside a priority. Or, put up a bird feeder and watch the bird channel from the window. Use your senses to observe your surroundings. Tune in to the sights, colors, sounds, birds, rustle, and movement of the leaves, feel of the breeze, warm or cool air, the texture of the trees. Being present in nature and connecting to this balanced and grounded frame of mind provides a window into the state of calm that we strive for throughout our day. When we tune into and appreciate peace, we train our minds and bodies to seek peace.

Pet therapy

Taking care of and interacting with cats and dogs is credited with reduced anxiety and stress.[24] Furry friends help us feel less lonely, and dogs can help keep us active. Pets can be a source of self-care for both caregiver and loved-one, adding joy to the lives of everyone who encounters them. Fish aquariums have worked to calm patients in doctor's office waiting rooms for years. An aquarium might be a lovely addition to your home environment. Birds can provide hours of entertainment. Pets require care, supplies, and add to the cleaning responsibilities, but you may decide that the payoff is well worth the cost.

Treat yourself

Get a coffee or ice cream while running errands. Plan the break between the appointments, shopping, and many tasks that keep you on the move. A coffee break may also offer a welcomed opportunity to spend time with your family member in a space with a different view where the conversation can be varied and non-care focused. When you connect with your family member in a new setting, it can reset the stress and remind you why you are so invested in this role.

---

24 Andrea Beetz, Kerstin Uvnäs-Moberg, Henri Julius and Kurt Kotrschal, "Psychosocial and psychophysiological effects of human-animal interactions: the possible role of oxytocin," *Frontiers in psychology*, 3 (2012): 234. https://doi.org/10.3389/fpsyg.2012.00234

Read
Download that book that will offer an escape or allow you to learn about something new. Books provide an opportunity to help us stay curious, get outside of ourselves, dig deeper, go on an adventure, or take a class without leaving home. Keep a book of short stories or meditations in your cozy corner and read a few a day. A book like The Daily Stoic[25] offers bite-sized portions of wisdom that inspire reflection and are ideal for a 5-minute self-care break.

Friends
Schedule a lunch or coffee with friends. Focus on reconnecting and catching up. It is important to note that friends don't always "get it" when it comes to caregiving stress. Expectations of empathy can be met with disappointment, but it can be the perfect opportunity to connect with life outside of caregiving.

Laugh
Appreciate the humor in those things that you know you will laugh about later. Watch a favorite comedy rerun, a funny movie, or a stand-up routine. Immerse yourself in whatever makes you smile out loud.

---

25   Ryan Holiday, *The Daily Stoic: 366 Meditations on Wisdom, Perseverance, and the Art of Living,* (Portfolio, October 18, 2016)

Knit, sew, or crochet
There are many YouTube channels that teach practically anything you would like to learn. There are oodles of books to inspire creativity. If you have ever wanted to take up knitting, this is a great time to pick up the needles and give it a go, getting lost in the rhythm of the process. You could create a gift for a member of your care team, your family member, or yourself.

Learn a new language or cuisine
A few minutes a day of study and practice prepares you to immerse yourself in the culture of a country you will visit in the future. You might also prepare a few dishes from your future destination. Imagine the adventure. Check out the Duolingo app for a great way to learn in 5 minutes a day.

A warm bath
Lighting, essential oils, Epsom salts, and a hydrating beverage can add to the calming effects of a nice soak. A warm bath relaxes the tense muscles that result from stress. As your muscles relax, your mood will lift, and the anxiety melts away.

The Value of a Routine

Routines are the glue that help you organize and prioritize the most critical activities, such as the self-care practices that make up your support system. Initially, I actively resisted a routine. A routine meant I was locked in, locked into the role, and locked into the obligation. It signified the loss of spontaneity, the loss of control over how I spent my time, the loss of freedom. Once I accepted the routine, I accepted full responsibility, and the tether would tighten, so I resisted.

I learned the value of a routine when my health suffered from neglecting my well-being. I found family caregiving and weight management to be mutually exclusive. Caregiving was stressful. Comfort food was comforting. It was also fast and filling, which was precisely what I reached for when I was overwhelmed and juggling so many tasks. My strategy was simply to stay alive. It was survival eating, but it was killing me. Blood pressure and bloodwork results confirmed that my food choices were compounding the toll that stress was taking on my body. Menopause and middle age had already done a number on my mid-section, and I needed a new plan. I decided to make a change. I created a list of protein intense foods and kept them handy for snacks. I ate based on a schedule, hungry or not.

By adhering to a routine, I regained my power. My mood, mind, and body were back within my control. I was inspired, and I added more routines into the day. When I was proactive and kept to the routines, I was better able to prioritize, I could act rather than react, and at the end of the day, I had more time for myself. In this way, I freed up my mind and time for creativity and self-care. It was tempting to discard the routines when unexpected events changed our course, but instead, I learned to identify routine disrupters and make modifications to keep the core components of the system in place, which helped me get through more turbulent times.

 Strategies in Sync: Self-care, Routines, Boundaries, Forgiveness, Compassion, Accept help, Mindfulness, Journaling, Venting

Each strategy is a form of self-care.

- Accept and Reframe: When we reframe negative thoughts, we become calm and focused. The act of reframing is self-care.
- Forgiveness: When we redirect our thoughts from a focus on unjust behaviors to a focus on compassion, we use our energy in ways that support our well-being. The act of forgiveness is self-care because it frees up our time and thoughts for self-care.
- Boundaries and Routines: Because boundaries help us prioritize and protect self-care, the act of setting boundaries, and boundaries around routines, is self-care.
- Self-compassion: Showing ourselves kindness and compassion is self-care. When we regularly practice compassion and, importantly, self-compassion, we build compassion muscles.

- Journaling and Venting: Letting it out by writing or talking are strategies that help us release pressure and process our complicated emotions. In this way, both strategies are a form of self-care.
- Mindfulness: Cultivating mindfulness and awareness trains our body and mind to relax. Taking time for meditation, breathing exercises, walks in nature, or any other activities that allow us to focus on the present moment are self-care.
- Planning: Shifting the focus from the worries to the solutions is empowering. It frees up our minds and our time to focus on our well-being and self-care activities.

Reflect

- Which self-care activities speak to you? What is missing?
- What do you consider guilty pleasures? What if you removed the guilt?
- What are your passions? How can you work your vital self-care interests into your daily activities?

Journal

- What do you miss from pre-caregiving days? As caregivers, we experience many losses. You might miss travel, time with friends, leisurely weekends.
- How can you care for yourself by creating experiences within your day that help you feel fulfilled

and connected to the hobbies that you have put on hold?

Practice

- Choose one or two activities mentioned in this chapter and layer in more as you redefine and re-claim self-care.
- Work your favorites into a routine and set boundaries to protect the time.

5 CULTIVATE COMPASSION & FORGIVENESS: LET LOVE RELEASE THE ANCHOR

Practice love, compassion, and forgiveness. Anger is nothing but an anchor that keeps you from moving forward.

ABBY FABIASCHI,
I LIKED MY LIFE

FEELING AND SHOWING compassion to ourselves and others becomes challenging as we begin to give more and more of our time and energy to caregiving tasks, responsibilities, and worries. When we practice compassion and forgiveness, we reduce and manage the stress of caring for a family member. When we forgive ourselves, family members, systems, and our care recipient, we free up our mind space for more positive and productive pursuits. Forgiveness and compassion allow us to maintain relationships and minimize stress and regret, which keeps us on course for a more sustainable caregiving experience.

First, we will discuss compassion, including self-compassion. Next, we'll explore forgiveness, including the importance of forgiving ourselves.

Compassion

Compassion is about giving all the love that you've got.

CHERYL STRAYED,
*TINY BEAUTIFUL THINGS: ADVICE ON
LOVE AND LIFE FROM DEAR SUGAR*

Compassion is showing kindness during difficult times. Consistent stress from caregiving can cause burnout resulting in more pressure because our coping mechanisms are no longer effective at restoring our energy. In this state, we are more easily overwhelmed and more quickly irritated. We often have trouble sleeping, which adds to the negative cycle. Feeling empathy drains us even further, and we no longer feel compassion for our care recipient, friends, family, strangers, or ourselves. Love feels elusive.

When we hear about caregivers who feel tremendous gratitude for the opportunity to care for a family member, it can feel like another failure on our part. If we experience burnout or compassion fatigue, gratitude is often not within the realm of possible emotions.

Whether we are experiencing burnout, empathic distress, or compassion fatigue - a type of post-traumatic stress disorder (PTSD) - we may look into the mirror and wonder who we have become. Returning to our compassionate selves requires that we identify the path that led us to our current state and then change direction. As part of that process, we may:

- Re-define and increase self-care activities
- Adjust boundaries or routines so that self-care is a priority and is protected
- Decide to add more help or try a different type of assistance
- Reevaluate venting opportunities.

Once we find what works for us, our compassion reserves - our ability to feel and show compassion - are replenished. It can be like putting on glasses with a new prescription, but instead of seeing things clearly again, we feel things clearly again.

The Compassion Fatigue Awareness Project offers the following definition: "Compassion fatigue is a broadly defined concept that can include emotional, physical, and spiritual distress in those providing care to another. It is associated with caregiving where people or animals are experiencing significant emotional or physical pain and suffering."[26] The Merriam-Webster dictionary describes compassion fatigue as, "Apathy or indifference toward the

---

26 "What is Compassion Fatigue?", Compassion Fatigue Awareness Project, accessed November 10, 2021, https://compassionfatigue.org/index.html

suffering of others as the result of overexposure to tragic news stories and images and the subsequent appeals for assistance."[27]

Burnout includes feelings of exhaustion of physical or emotional strength or motivation, usually due to prolonged stress or frustration. Other research indicates that empathy, rather than compassion, fatigues.[28] Tania Singer, psychologist and social neuroscientist and Olga Klimecki, psychologist and neuroscientist, describe empathic distress as, "A strong aversive and self-oriented response to the suffering of others, accompanied by the desire to withdraw from a situation in order to protect oneself from excessive negative feelings."[29]

Compassion stimulates areas of love and connectedness in the brain.[30] Empathy triggers pain regions.[31] Tension results when we feel the pull of compassion yet distance ourselves from the suffering that comes with

---

[27] Merriam-Webster, s.v. "compassion fatigue", accessed November 10, 2021, https://www.merriam-webster.com/dictionary/compassion%20fatigue

[28] Trisha Dowling, "Compassion does not fatigue!" *The Canadian veterinary journal = La revue veterinaire canadienne*, 59, no. 7 (2018), 749–750.

[29] Tania Singer, Olga M. Klimecki, "Empathy and Compassion", *Current Biology*, 24, no. 18, 22 (2014): R875-R878, *https://doi.org/10.1016/j.cub.2014.06.054*

[30] Tobias Esch, and George B. Stefano, "The neurobiological link between compassion and love," *Medical science monitor: international medical journal of experimental and clinical research*, 17, no. 3 (2011): RA65–RA75. https://doi.org/10.12659/msm.881441

[31] Tania Singer et al., "Empathy for pain involves the affective but not sensory components of pain," *Science (New York, N.Y.)*, 303, no. 5661 (2004): 1157–1162. https://doi.org/10.1126/science.1093535

empathy, two competing instincts. It is distressing. When we choose to move toward and into the uncomfortable space, it is compassion that grounds us, then propels us into action. Acting with compassion strengthens our compassion muscles because compassion is not only innate but is learnable and contagious. A Buddhist definition of compassion is, "When love meets suffering and stays loving." We instinctively distance ourselves from suffering. When we act with compassion, we turn toward suffering, lean into it. We face fear and decide we can handle it.

As caregivers we face many common barriers that impede us from acting with compassion, including exhaustion, anger, resentment, and fear. When our boundaries are consistently crossed, these barriers increase in number and intensity. As kids, we ooze compassion. As caregivers, it can feel like our compassion has all oozed out. This leaves us feeling empty and angry and wondering who we have become.

Compassion fatigue can occur when caregiver stress has gone so far that it affects our overall ability to feel compassion, not just for our care recipient but for anyone, including ourselves. We could say that healthy boundaries are inspired by compassion; compassion for ourselves, compassion for our care recipient, and compassion for those who help us care for our family member. Compassion helps us reinforce our boundaries in a way that maintains relationships and, in doing so, helps us maintain an overall sense of well-being. Boundaries help us protect our compassion reserves by establishing limits that prevent a build-up of resentment and anger.

Imagine your compassion reserves are in a blue heart-shaped pillow, and you are hugging this pillow. It gives you comfort, and you are protecting it. You are holding your compassion and sitting in a fluffy cloud, a cloud of calm and clarity. The cloud boundaries shift. You can't see or touch them, but they are there, protecting you and your compassion reserves. Outside the cloud is the chaos of life, but the area within the circle around you remains calm because the boundaries work to protect your compassion reserves. When someone starts to cross your boundary, channel the Rolling Stones and say, "Hey, You, Get off of my Cloud," but say it with compassion.

In the moment, when the emotions are swirling, imagine giving yourself a big hug. You deserve it. This is hard. Ask yourself the question, "What do I need in this moment?" Take a few deep breaths and sit with that question. You could then ask, "What do we need in this moment?" These questions will lead us to compassion. If we can be compassionate with ourselves while feeling these powerful emotions, the barriers mentioned earlier dissipate. We can then accept our situation, our challenges, and our shortcomings. We can more clearly see the compassionate way forward.

Practicing self-compassion shows yourself the consideration and care that you would give a friend who was going through a challenging experience. Showing ourselves kindness and compassion fosters our resilience and ability to cope with the challenges of caregiving. There are many ways to show kindness to yourself, beginning with your thoughts. Negative self-talk can sabotage us and create more stress. When we feel inadequate and reinforce the feelings with negative self-talk about our perceived lack of abilities or mistakes, we can misread others' motivations and interpret them through the lens of our negativity. We can miss the bright side because we are so focused on the dark side. Negative self-talk can lead to ruminating and excessive worrying. We can stop negative self-talk in its tracks with awareness and replace it with a positive mantra. We can also use mindfulness to explore the validity of the thought and, with clarity, reframe the challenge that caused the negative thoughts. If you find that you are self-critical, you may consider the advice or comfort or kind words you would offer a friend who was in a similar situation. Maybe even write those words of wisdom in your journal.

Another way to show yourself compassion is to take a break when you are feeling stressed and overwhelmed. We often feel guilt when we aren't managing a situation well, and taking a break might add to the guilt, but it is what we need and what we deserve. We may also use this break as an opportunity to reframe the experience. We can ask ourselves what we have learned and how we might benefit from the difficulty.

Self-compassion permits us to engage in self-care. If self-care is a new concept and it feels selfish, showing compassion for ourselves will help us recognize that caring for ourselves is not selfish. With self-compassion, we detach guilt from self-care and attach respect.

Self-compassion isn't the same as feeling sorry for ourselves. Instead, it is about feeling empowered. For example, we might enter a challenging situation with an intention to maintain our sense of wholeness and courage. We acknowledge that this is hard, and we will feel challenged, and we owe ourselves space and grace to feel the emotions and the opportunity to grow from the struggle. Let compassion be your compass.

Reflect

- Reflect forward. Imagine that you have developed a foundation of mindfulness, cultivated self-compassion, and are direct and honest in communicating boundaries.
- How does the caregiving experience look different than the current situation?

Journal

- Consider this quote widely attributed to Rumi, "Never give from the depths of your well, but from your overflow."[32] Describe what it feels like to be low on love, to be giving from the depths of your well.

---

32 Rachel Williams, "The Caregiver's Guide to Self-Care: Part I," Chopra, March 21, 2017, https://chopra.com/articles/the-caregivers-guide-to-self-care-part-i

- Starting with yourself, how can you begin to replenish your well?

Practice
- Ask yourself each day, as often as necessary, "What do I need to replenish my feelings of well-being?"
- "If your compassion doesn't include yourself, it is incomplete."[33] Using this quote as inspiration, develop a mantra and place it prominently as a reminder to fill your well throughout the day.

Forgiveness

Anger, resentment and jealousy doesn't change the heart of others – it only changes yours.

SHANNON ALDER,

300 QUESTIONS TO ASK YOUR PARENTS BEFORE IT'S TOO LATE

It is possible to spend an enormous amount of time and energy on anger and resentment. As caregivers, we often have a legitimate list of people, events, systems, and services that have failed us. The problem with resentment is that it eats away at us from the inside. When we forgive, we

---

33 Jack Kornfield, *Buddha's Little Instruction Book*, (Bantam Books, 1994), 28.

release guilt and resentment. We are not condoning what has occurred, but we are no longer defined by the wrongs that have been committed. We can acknowledge and feel the pain, accept what has happened and decide to let the resentment and the pain go. Our hearts feel lighter when we no longer carry the burden of anxiety and negative emotions.

The practice of forgiveness has been connected to improved emotional and physical health, including a positive impact on sleep and stress reduction.[34] There is evidence that a daily practice of forgiveness can lower heart rate and blood pressure.[35] We may not be aware of how often our thoughts turn to old grudges. We may realize that our body tenses or we may hold our breath briefly. This physical reaction to dwelling on a grievance takes a toll. The stress hormone cortisol is released. When this happens repeatedly, our hormones adjust over time, and the shift can cause depression. To deal with the stress caused by ruminating, we may engage in destructive behaviors or unhealthy avoidance activities that lead to further decline in our health. When we release the negative feelings through forgiveness, the opposite happens, and the hormones that support happiness and feelings of well-being are released.[36]

---

34 "Forgiveness: Your Health Depends on It," *Johns Hopkins Medicine*, accessed November 10, 2021, https://www.hopkinsmedicine.org/health/wellness-and-prevention/forgiveness-your-health-depends-on-it

35 Johns Hopkins Medicine, "Forgiveness: Your Health Depends on It."

36 Dariush Dfarhud, Maryam Malmir and Mohammad Khanahmadi, Happiness & Health: The Biological Factors- Systematic Review Article. *Iranian journal of public health*, 43 no. 11 (2014): 1468–1477.

The list of who and what to forgive will be as unique as each family caregiver and their circumstances. We can start with ourselves and let guilt be our guide. Our care recipient may inspire us to forgive past, present, and future grievances. Siblings and close family members may have let you down. While systems may have been broken, the helpers in the systems are not the systems themselves. It is important not to confuse the limitations of the process with the people who are a part of the process.

In the same way, society can be helpful and hindering at the same time. Our employer systems may have caused us grief. While the list ebbs and flows as the experience intensifies, we can acknowledge the lessons and growth that we experience from each act of forgiveness.

When I assessed how I might forgive myself, I recognized that I felt guilty for being reactive, deficiently proactive, making mistakes, and misunderstanding. I realized that forgiveness had to start with self-compassion. I began to include reflection in my journal whenever I felt regret. My journal prompt to get started was, "I made a mistake. What next? How can I learn from what happened?" Honest reflection helped me put the incident in perspective, understand why I behaved in a particular way and the role others' actions, or reactions may have played. I tried to understand underlying factors that contributed to my mishandling of an interaction. Was I tired, hungry, or both? Could I have taken a break that might have prevented the pressure that built up throughout the day? Journaling the insights, lessons learned, and changes needed allowed me to shift from self-criticism to a place of empowerment. Resilience came when I acknowledged that I did the best I could, and now I had information that would help me do better the next time.

Next, I had to forgive Dad for the past, present, and future. I was angry and resentful because Dad struggled with these exact feelings when caring for his mom but did not take action or initiate a conversation to prevent me from this similar fate. I was angry because Dad made it difficult to be his caregiver by resisting both help and reason, admittedly my side of the story. Forgiving my brother for his lack of involvement in our father's care coincided with feelings of gratitude that he did not interfere. My brother was not critical or judgmental. He was doing the best he could, just like I was, and that had to be good enough.

When we have determined who and what to forgive, we may need to learn how to forgive. Robert Enright, the author of Forgiveness is a Choice: A Step-by-Step Process for Resolving Anger and Restoring Hope, suggests that we need to become "forgivingly fit."[37] To do this, we need to train our forgiving heart muscles and practice small acts of forgiveness. The first step in the forgiveness process is to feel the hurt. We can describe the pain in our journal. We can analyze why it is painful, what we have learned from the experience, and how we have changed. The second step is to further reflect

---

37   Robert Enright, "Eight Keys to Forgiveness," *Greater Good Magazine*, October 15, 2015, https://greatergood.berkeley.edu/article/item/eight_keys_to_forgiveness

on why the offense occurred. Assess the event from all perspectives, including from the offender's point of view. When we can understand that we are all limited by our conditioning, we may realize that we all do our best given our circumstances, ego constraints, and personal limits. Finally, we need to detach from the story. That doesn't mean that we forget, but that the memory no longer inspires negative emotion.

Opportunities to practice forgiveness present themselves organically through the day, and with mindfulness and awareness, we can recognize them and take advantage of the opportunities to be more compassionate. It may be that we refrain from saying something disparaging or that we offer kind words during a moment of frustration. Whether active or passive practice, small daily acts will help us become more skilled at demonstrating empathy and forgiveness, which are closely connected. Practice will help us rewire our brains to be prepared to undertake more challenging forgiveness opportunities. Mindfulness and forgiveness share another connection. When we practice forgiveness, we cut our ties to the past and place our attention on the present as we let go of what no longer serves us.

Caregiving responsibilities are complex, and mistakes are inevitable. Forgiving ourselves is equally essential to forgiving others who we believe have let us down. We are often navigating complex systems under emotionally charged circumstances. It is common to feel like we aren't strong enough or smart enough to manage the challenges.

We can be hard on ourselves when things do not go as planned. Dwelling on our mistakes can cause us to lose sleep and suffer from the other adverse effects of stress. Resilience and self-forgiveness are crucial so that we continue with confidence.

When we have followed the steps of forgiveness, we can conclude a situation by expressing that we did our best with the resources that were available to us, focusing on the heart and saying the words, "I forgive you." Celebrate what you have learned from the experience. Feel gratitude for the lesson and growth.

Strategies in Sync: Compassion, Forgiveness, Mindfulness, Boundaries, Self-care

Developing strong compassion and forgiveness muscles fortifies our resilience and keeps us focused on solutions, including maintaining our well-being.

- Mindfulness: A focus on the present moment will allow us to act with compassion rather than react with the negative energy that accompanies negative thoughts and emotions.
- Boundaries: Awareness will help us recognize the damage caused by staying stuck in the mud so that we can set boundaries around how much time we will spend focused on resentment, anger and unforgiveness.

- Self-care: When we honor these limits and practice compassion, self-compassion, and forgiveness, we free up our hearts and minds to focus on love and well-being. In this way, compassion and forgiveness are self-care practices.

Reflect

- When have you felt injured, and by whom?
- Does this event take up space in your mind?
- How would it feel to be at peace?
- *"True forgiveness is when you can say, 'Thank you for that experience.'"*[38] – Oprah Winfrey. Is there a gift within the forgiveness?

Journal

- What have you done that you might forgive?
- Why do you deserve to be forgiven?
- Who else can you forgive? Describe how each act of forgiveness might unfold.

Practice

- Feel the release that comes from letting go of the burden of blame.
- Look for opportunities to apply empathy and compassion and forgive yourself and others before focusing on the injury consumes a disproportionate amount of thought.

---

38 Monica Chon, "25 Forgiveness Quotes to Help You Let Go of the Past," *Oprah Daily*, Aug 11, 2021, https://www.oprahdaily.com/life/relationships-love/g29995262/forgiveness-quotes/?slide=6

6 RELEASE THE EMOTIONS: WATERFALLS LEAD TO RAINBOWS

Unleash in the right time and place before you explode at the wrong time and place.

OLI ANDERSON,
PERSONAL REVOLUTIONS: A SHORT COURSE IN REALNESS

IT IS CRUCIAL to be able to express emotions from events that cause you stress. The act of sharing or venting is a release that makes you feel lighter and less burdened. The key is to locate a listener who gets what you are going through, someone who has been through a similar experience. A regular practice of venting, worked into your routine, will help prevent the stressors from creating layers of trauma that will add to the overwhelm. Letting out the frustrations and, frankly, the fears is a must, because caregiving is sustainable when we believe that we can not only survive but thrive in our role. One or more of the options below can offer an opportunity to unload, receive essential validation, connect, and know that you are not alone.

Support groups can provide a chance to communicate with various caregivers who can relate to the challenges and the stresses of caregiving. It is vital to locate a support group that is a good fit for you. There are disease-specific support groups, grieving support groups, and many more in-person and virtual meetings available. When looking for a support group that is a good fit, you may encounter different formats. Some are run by professionals such as a social worker or therapist, and others are run by group members. Some have guest speakers. Some groups have themes for each meeting, and others flow from the needs of the group. Find the specific meeting frequency that works best for you. There may be a fee. Begin your search with your local Area Agency on Aging. If your care recipient has been diagnosed with a disease, go to websites that offer support and advocacy. Look for local chapter information or virtual support group options. There are links to some of these groups on the resources page of the websites.

A key to feeling supported is to acknowledge that you will receive the best support from someone who has experienced similar losses due to caregiving. While you may learn much from someone whose care recipient has had a similar disease diagnosis, you will also connect with members based on the impact that you have experienced. For example, if you loved to travel and can no longer travel due to increasing care responsibilities, support and validation will come from someone who has been impacted similarly.

In-person Support Group
Support groups offer benefits beyond venting that will help you find your sustainable path. Support group members have experienced challenges similar to yours and therefore may have solutions to offer. Resources such as websites, agencies, and books are shared. You likely will discover new coping strategies and find the hope that felt elusive due to the overwhelming struggles. You should expect to feel more empowered and confident as your care recipient's advocate when you find your voice among your peers. You can feel relief when your frustrations are not just understood but validated. Learning and sharing with others in a safe space will help you explore your thoughts, emotions, reactions, fears, and options. Just knowing that you are not alone can be the most significant benefit of attending support group meetings. Helping others has its own feel-good benefits.

Virtual Support Group
There are online Facebook support groups for caregivers; each has a unique focus, such as caring for elderly parents, dementia, caring for children with special needs, and more. These groups offer an opportunity to share specific challenges and receive advice. They allow you to see the difficulties others face, know that you are not alone, and

benefit from the other members' advice. You may reach out to members for advice, use the opportunity to share what has worked for you, or just offer empathy to another facing a familiar struggle. On the other hand, reading about other caregivers' struggles and the comments may cause more overwhelm. Written communication presents challenges when interpreting tone and empathy. Advice and opinions may be offered in ways that feel judgmental, disrespectful, and not supportive. As with all stress-relieving resources, a virtual support group may serve you well during specific segments of the caregiving journey and during other parts may need to be set aside for later consideration.

Professional Support

A professional such as a counselor, therapist, clergy member, or caregiver coach may be a good option to vent and receive support, but as with many aspects of caregiving, trial and error will lead you to the best solution for your situation. It is crucial to find a good fit, and it may take working with a few different people before you find the best match. It is important that you like the person with whom you are working. It is equally essential that you trust this individual. Trust means that you can be open without feeling judged so that you can get to the core of the concern. It may be that a counselor's connection to care is helpful, or you may find that it alters the interaction in a way that is not helpful. Is the gender, age, or religious affiliation of the therapist a critical factor?

There are many online options available, and you are not limited to working with someone in your vicinity.

Think about the objectives you would like to accomplish with coaching, counseling, or therapy so that you can discuss the goals and how together you will reach them. Would you like to focus on your emotions and reactions or delve more into communication and relating challenges between you and your care recipient or members of your care team? Problem solving or locating resources may be the most immediate need.

A caregiving coach may appeal to you because they have been in your shoes and can relate to much of your experience. Many of them began working with family caregivers because they were overwhelmed and felt hopeless. They were able to reach a place where they were navigating their experience well and now want to help others who are on their own caregiving journey. They can provide resources and insights on how to manage the complicated family dynamics that accompany caregiving. Caregiving is stressful whether you provide direct care on-site, live fifteen minutes away, or live several states away. A caregiver coach can help with strategies to manage stress, and they understand the value of self-care and the difficulty of incorporating self-care into a day of caregiving.

Friend or Relative

A friend or relative who has cared for a family member might offer support that actually feels supportive. If someone has not been in a similar situation, they likely won't get it and simply cannot relate to caregiving's complexity. For this reason, we often experience distance between family and friends to whom we may have been previously close. This is a challenging aspect of caregiving and contributes to loneliness. Resentment can surface when we feel abandoned. It is helpful to understand that we all have limitations and then adjust our expectations accordingly. If friends and family aren't able to lend a supportive ear, there may be other ways that they can help. Be specific in your requests and be prepared to accept that you may need to resume your relationship when caregiving responsibilities change. Forgiveness serves us well when we feel a lack of support and have been let down by our inner circle.

Journaling

Journaling thoughts and exploring them with curiosity and objectivity is a form of venting and can be therapeutic. Self-reflection throughout the caregiving experience can be healing. It provides raw self-awareness, which can help when our sensitivities are heightened due to stress combined with feelings of guilt, anger, and resentment. Denise M. Brown, author of The Caregiving Years: Six Stages to a Meaningful Journey, interviewed *B. Lynn Goodwin* in a podcast titled, Writing your Caregiving

Journey. Ms. Goodwin shares that while caring for her mom, she used her journal as a place to put her anger. Support groups did not work for her, but journaling did. She began coaching family caregivers in the journaling process and saw many start from a place of anger or frustration and move to a place of grace through their writing. In her words, she "wanted others to have a safe place where they could dump the outrage, where they could write and know it's not true as they're writing it."[39]

Lynn does not read her journals from that time in her life. Many of us can relate. We feel shame about these emotions and a journal is a safe place to store them. However, you may decide to read your journals. If so, you can look back with self-compassion and clarity that comes from distance. This process can be reaffirming and help you process that transformational part of your life.

Keeping a journal also can enable you to process caregiving's complexities, the emotions, the fear, and the confusion. Writing offers a release and reprieve from the swirling sensations. It can help you capture the fun and funny moments. You will have a record of the experience, a travel journal that documents the caregiving journey. It will shine a light on the growth and how far you have traveled along the caregiver river. The opportunity to reflect can help you stay focused and productive during

---

39 B. Lynn Goodwin, "Writing your Caregiving Journey", from a podcast hosted by Denise M. Brown, *https://www.blogtalkradio.com/caregiving/2008/10/04/Writing-Your-Caregiving-Journey* (podcast no longer accesible)

a time when both focus and productivity fluctuate from minute to minute. You will be able to look back at this time and remember what it felt like, what it looked like, how you spent your time. A record of this transformation will be a powerful reminder of your strength.

Documenting the experience can take any form. Your journal may be a spreadsheet, a handwritten or typed diary, a photoblog, videos, drawings, or any combination that will allow you to capture the story. If you are not sure where to start, just start writing and see where it goes. There is no right or wrong way to write. Let your thoughts and words flow like a raging river, a gentle stream, or a waterfall spilling and splashing onto the page.

Another valuable use for journaling is to note moments of gratitude. You can start small, and each evening, list one or two reasons for gratitude that are in some way connected to caregiving. As you begin to perceive more and more opportunities to feel grateful, your list will grow. Once you see gratitude, it can't be unseen, and the experience can be transforming.

Journaling is empowering when we write about wounds and the process of healing. The act of journaling is a part of the healing practice. Our journal becomes a beautiful reflection of our experience and our journey.

Strategies in Sync: Journaling, Venting, Self-care, Routines, Mindfulness, Forgiveness, Boundaries, Compassion, Accept help, Planning

Venting and journaling work together with each of the strategies because when we process our thoughts and the circumstances that led to stressful events, we can make adjustments that will improve our situation and ultimately our well-being.

- Self-care: Journaling and verbally communicating the challenges are self-care activities that allow you to release the built-up pressure from stress.
- Mindfulness: Awareness will facilitate processing our thoughts and emotions so that we learn and grow from the challenges. When we learn and grow, we can more easily move with the flow of our experience.
- Forgiveness: Grudges can be a source of stress and frustration that keep us distracted and focused on negative thoughts. When, through conversation or writing, we work through our thoughts about who and what to forgive, we lighten our emotional load.
- Boundaries: When we share our experiences verbally or in writing, we process each experience in a different way. With perspective, we may iden-

tify where new or modified boundaries may serve to better protect our well-being.
- Compassion: Opportunities for compassion become evident when we process the events that caused us and others pain. We can journal about our need to express and feel self-compassion.

Reflect

- How do you currently release your frustrations and how do you feel after you share the challenges, the difficulties?
- What options have you considered and not yet tried?
- If you were to keep a journal of your caregiving journey, what form would it take? Would it include anecdotes, an exploration of emotions, poetry? Would it be handwritten, typed, kept on an app, photos, video?

Journal

- Your negative emotions are normal and natural and very painful. Begin to identify and explore the negative emotions that come to the surface throughout the day.
- Write about a challenging episode and describe how you felt before, during, and after the interaction. Reflection may provide a different perspective or helpful insight.

Practice

- If you are currently using a method to vent that is working well, incorporate it into a routine, and protect the practice with boundaries to let it out consistently.
- If you have not yet found an effective method of venting, select one of the options and begin to experiment to discover what works best for you to achieve a release and feel empowered.
- If you haven't done so already, choose a journal and begin to record your caregiving journey. It is helpful to journal regularly. Incorporating journaling into a routine may help you achieve consistency.

PART II
SUSTAINABILITY STRATEGIES: THE PRACTICAL

To begin with the end in mind means to start with a clear understanding of your destination. It means to know where you're going so that you better understand where you are now and so that the steps you take are always in the right direction.

STEPHEN R. COVEY,

THE 7 HABITS OF HIGHLY EFFECTIVE PEOPLE

7 TIMING THE TRANSITIONS: READ THE RIVER

The appeal of the wild for me is its unpredictability. You have to develop an awareness, react fast, be resourceful and come up with a plan and act on it.

BEAR GRYLLS,
BEAR GRYLLS SURVIVAL ACADEMY FACEBOOK PAGE

THE LANDSCAPE OF a familiar river can change which modifies the flow and speed of the current. Awareness - reading the river - is the key to identifying when a change is needed because heightened awareness will help us recognize when we need to modify our actions based on the unique setting.

How do we know when it is no longer safe for Mom or Dad to live alone? When is it no longer safe for Mom or Dad to continue driving, or when should we step in to help manage finances or medications? These questions demonstrate concern for our parent's safety and are often juxtaposed against our parent's fiercely held desire for independence. In addition to being emotionally charged, the answers have enormous ramifications for us as the family caregiver.

How could this play out? Suppose Mom has fallen a few times and fortunately sustained only scratches and bruises. Her home is usually immaculate, and the refrigerator well-stocked and organized. Lately though, dust and clutter remain untouched, and expired food fills the fridge shelves. Mom has managed finances on her own, and you know little about the status of her financial affairs. Recently, you noticed a few past due payment notifications sitting on the kitchen table. If we read the river, we see that another fall may result in a hospitalization. What changes could be made in the home to create safer spaces? Spoiled food may soon cause an illness. It is time for help with meals and housekeeping. A banking error, or even more concerning, fraud, is possibly on the horizon. We can begin to ask questions about finances, learn the status of credit card accounts, and identify the locations of bank accounts and insurance policy paperwork. We can prepare to monitor and eventually take over the responsibility of bill paying. Ideally, the conversation about the available options will take place long before the need presents itself. Unfortunately, these difficult conversations are often avoided until a decision is urgent.

Prior planning and preparation, knowing the options, and having conversations early help us move forward with confidence when concerns surface. You may research worries and possible solutions online. Another option is to find a guide, talk to someone who has experience navigating the caregiver river, ideally a current or former family caregiver. You might reach out to health care professionals for information and guidance to understand better what the future holds. Planning, preparation, and awareness will reduce the anxiety that comes with change and empower you as you navigate through the transitions. Conversations with your family member will help you determine when and how to make direction changes. Tips and strategies for having care conversations are covered in chapter 8.

Legal and Financial Matters

As soon as you become aware that you may be involved in a family member's care, no matter how far in the future, consult with an attorney and/or financial advisor who can help explain and coordinate the documents that could be necessary for your family's situation. Online legal sites such as LegalZoom and Nolo can be consulted. Powers of Attorney (POA's) should be established. A Healthcare POA (also called a Medical POA) designates a proxy to make medical decisions in case of incapacity and to communicate with the patient's doctor to ensure treatment wishes are honored. The person designated to make these decisions is called the attorney-in-fact. As a caregiver, you will want to know your loved one's wishes. A POA designation will provide health care and medical professionals the documentation needed to accept the decisions you make on your loved one's behalf. A power of attorney designates an agent or attorney-in-fact to represent your loved one regarding financial, personal, or business matters. A durable power of attorney stays in effect should your loved one become incapacitated. A general power of attorney would no longer be valid under those circumstances. Your caregiver responsibilities will likely evolve to managing bank accounts, paying bills, following up on health insurance claims, and more. You will be required to provide power-of-attorney documentation before a representative will discuss your family member's personal or business details.

Warning signs that indicate that help with finances is needed include accumulated unopened mail, past-due notifications, or frequent credit card company calls. Another warning sign is when your parent isn't able to answer questions about the status of their accounts. If spending habits change, you notice abnormally large purchases or less frequent grocery shopping, further investigation may reveal confusion or cognitive changes. One of the the first places dementia may be discovered is in the bank account. An important reason to take action before an event such as a hospitalization or illness diagnosis is to avoid the complications and cost of getting a POA when a family member is incapacitated and can no longer designate a proxy.

Well before I connected to the term, I unknowingly began functioning in the caregiver role. Mom had passed eight years earlier, and she was still listed on Dad's bank account. There were credit cards in her name, which signaled that I should look into what else was happening with Dad's finances. He welcomed adding me onto his accounts, and I became the primary attorney-in-fact. This designation allowed me to interact with the insurance company and other institutions on his behalf when we had questions about bills or coverage. As I began to take over bill paying, taxes, and shopping, the transitions were less complicated with a POA in place.

End-of-Life planning
End-of-life is the ultimate transition. Before the need is imminent, the topics to discuss include:

- Preparing a will.
- Determining the need for and stipulations to be covered in an advance directive.
- Deciding on a cemetery and burial plot location.
- Funeral arrangements.

While it will come toward the end of your experience, if we begin with the end in mind, we begin by having conversations and making decisions that help us plan a scenario that brings a meaningful close to a meaningful journey. The series of discussions surrounding end-of-life can be daunting and emotional under the best of circumstances but are significantly more challenging when a serious diagnosis or a hospitalization requires decisions to be made. Begin to ask questions that will allow you to learn your family member's wishes, understand what planning has been completed and what steps are yet to be taken.

Housing and Safety

Sometimes, it quickly becomes evident that our family member is no longer safe living alone, and other times it is like asking a Magic 8-Ball to predict the future. The series of events that led me to realize that Dad could no longer live alone came fast and furious in the form of a house fire. Dad was 94. Joe and I were living in France. I talked to Dad three to four times a week. We had long conversations about current events, family, his health, our travels, what he was reading, and any number of topics. It seemed that he was still sharp and managing well, until the fire. He had a tray of 30+ candles that he lit most evenings. The last time he did this, he fell asleep on the sofa and awoke to a smoke-filled condo. The candles had burnt down through the tray, and the dresser was in flames. He had the presence of mind to get a towel, soak it and throw it over the dresser. The flames were extinguished.

When Dad shared that there had been a fire, he left out a few details. He neglected to share that the insurance company insisted that he stay elsewhere due to the excessive smoke and that they would pay for his accommodations, which he refused. Dad did not tell me that the damage required new flooring, walls to be painted, replacement of bedding and curtains, all totaling over $50K. He did not tell me that he was having trouble walking due to the slices in his feet from the exploded glass that had held many of the candles. Little by little, the details came out. This was the catalyst that eventually brought us back to the U.S.

Linda Burhans, The Gal Who Cares for Caregivers, tells the story of a daughter visiting her parents. Through a social chat with her parent's neighbor, she discovered that an ambulance had been to her parent's home the prior week and took her mom to the hospital. This was the first she had heard of it. Talk to your parent's neighbors. At the very least, you might give them your contact information in case they need to reach you.

Rather than wait for a fire or other disaster, the conversation regarding where your parent(s) would like to live in the future and what that might look like can begin when a life event or circumstance brings the question to the surface. For example, your parents may comment on the level of home maintenance required or the desire to downsize. You and your siblings may have relocated to different cities, and your parents may no longer have a deep connection to the community. You might notice that the layout or steps in their home present mobility challenges. The conversation may look different depending on when and why you begin, but it is never too early to start the discussion, ask the questions, learn the wishes, and plant the seeds of collaboration.

If safety is a concern, your plan might include cameras or a life alert system, safety bars, and better lighting. When a safety concern arises, take some time for research, trial, and error. Awareness can help you stay a step ahead of the mishaps, but not always. It is important to know that accidents will happen, which provides an opportunity to learn, forgive, and possibly prevent further casualties.

I avoided this topic with complete intention. I was confident that Dad would refuse to consider living in an assisted living facility. One of our adult relationship's biggest battles happened when I insisted that his mom go into a nursing home. Outside help could no longer handle my grandmother. She had been living with my parents for eleven years. Taking care of her became an extreme burden on my mom's well-being. Grandma was 101 years old, not frail, and she had dementia. Dad refused to discuss the option of moving to a care facility. I thought he and I would never speak again when I insisted that it was no longer safe for her to live with them. He finally relented, and his mom stayed in a nursing home for three years until she passed at the age of 104. Dad or Mom went to visit her every day, at first together, and then they alternated, each going every other day. They went at mealtime to help the staff by helping grandma eat. Dad did not like hospitals, and this nursing home felt very much like a hospital. He was completely, yet reluctantly, devoted.

Twenty years later, I knew that Dad expected the same level of "devotion" from me. I knew, but we hadn't discussed a plan for the time when Dad would need more help, wouldn't be able to live on his own. I mistakenly thought that when the time came, I could show Dad that the current care facility options were more like living in a coed dorm rather than in a hospital. Dad's primary care physician described a few as a constant party. Not even I fell for that sales job. I planned to wait until the time came because I believed getting a "no" early in the process would be a difficult obstacle to overcome. So, I waited and waited and waited. A plan to wait was not a plan.

Three years after Dad suffered and recovered from a stroke and with several systems in place, Joe and I moved out of his home but stayed close. I understood that something unfortunate could happen whether I was there or not. Once I'd done my best to minimize the risks, acceptance rather than obsession allowed our caregiving arrangement to be sustainable. I still spent two to three hours a day at his place managing his affairs, but it gave us all some much-needed space. Then, little by little, I noticed daily decisions and events that caused concern. Boiled eggs were blown up on the stove more than once. Dad illegally took the golf cart onto dangerous roads. He enjoyed talking to telemarketers and then became a victim of identity theft. Dad wasn't eating because he wanted to lose weight and then he passed out. He complained about his balance but regularly got on ladders. It felt like we were one incident away from serious consequences. As my time at Dad's increased to four to six hours a day, I often left feeling uncomfortable about what would transpire while I was gone. A year and a half after moving out, the decision to move back in wasn't as clear, but more oversight was clearly needed. We found the perfect home that would better accommodate the three of us. Dad looked at it, agreed it was ideal, and was ready to move for nine hours. Then, he refused with an intensity that shut the door permanently. The assisted living facility conversations had been had, deposits placed and returned, and "over his dead body" was his current position. We closed that door together because my reluctance for him to move was equal to his. His routine and lifestyle were so firmly established that I couldn't imagine him making the adjustment unless he were completely in agreement with the decision, and he wasn't.

Following our return from France, I wasted a few years on anger and resentment that swirled in a downward, spinning spiral of miscomprehension. My version of reality, the choice about where and how Joe and I were going to spend our 50's was out of our control and was founded on fear. Dad's version of reality was also based on fear. He was not able to imagine a change. It terrified him. Furthermore, he didn't need help. I needed to repeat that for myself. He didn't need help. He was managing just fine, and anything I offered was value-added, not necessary, and just nice to have. In his version of reality, Joe and I were free to live wherever we wanted. He was not wrong. The reality that Joe and I lived in, the one where we had seen the signs and knew we needed to be close, wasn't any more real than Dad's version. There was a reality in the middle.

While I am certain that it was not safe for Dad to live alone, I am not convinced that we should have moved back in with him. It closed off our options. We were doing so much for him that he could easily convince himself that he was independent when, in reality, he was managing very few of his affairs. At the very least, I wish we had had conversations about what the future might look like when he needed more help. I wish we had discussed the hardships that he endured while taking care of his mom and how we might approach his future more collaboratively.

Health and medical

Missed pills, a change in prescriptions, a mention of symptoms, or a disease diagnosis is an indicator to ask more questions and learn about health status, medications, and doctors. After the fire, I started to listen during my conversations with Dad through different ears. Joe and I made plans to return home from France. Once back, Dad was diagnosed with atrial fibrillation. This would not have happened if we were not there because he refused to wear the prescribed heart monitor and only relented after I had a complete meltdown. I was familiar with his stubbornness but perceived this refusal as a complete lack of responsibility. It was the first of many battles that left me baffled. Why was he using such poor judgment? He complained about his heart's frequent fluttering yet refused to follow the prescribed method to determine the cause. We moved forward with a pacemaker and new meds, including Coumadin/Warfarin, a blood thinner which was a real challenge to manage. Dad's blood had to be tested weekly to determine the proper dose. Week after week, we went to the lab and received disappointing results. Also, Dad was covered in bruises because of this medication. I resigned myself to our new reality. In hindsight, I wish I had researched newer, alternative blood thinners.

One night, he passed out three times and didn't tell me even though I was in the next room. I woke up when I heard him struggling to stand in his bathroom. I called 911. He had had a bleed because of the blood thinner. I didn't know what was happening. I thought he was dying. His return home was delayed because he had been given too much fluid and went into heart failure. Finally home and with the doctor's consent, he stopped taking Coumadin. Within weeks he had a stroke. This event put us in a terrible cycle: hospital, then rehab at a facility. Next, rehab at home and finally full recovery. After doing research and consulting more carefully with both Dad's cardiologist and his primary care physician, Eliquis replaced Coumadin as his new blood thinner.

I share these events because they highlight the gaps in hearing or understanding which made it clear that I needed to hear first-hand what each doctor said or suggested. I needed to ask questions so that Dad and I could both better understand the options and consequences. I needed to become a true care partner, which meant that I carry a list of Dad's medications, understand why each was prescribed, and know the side effects.

Suppose you are simply helping your parent with finances or running errands. Even in that case, you have already assumed the caregiving role and while healthcare may now be in maintenance mode at this point, it is still the appropriate time to meet your parent's physicians and begin to gain an understanding of their health condition, medications, and advice offered by the doctor. To ease the transition, you could ask to go to a scheduled visit to introduce yourself and establish a relationship. It is nice to have this conversation and to have met for the first time under calm circumstances. This setting allows you to ask your parent if they like their doctors and why. You can also ask about their medicines and how they manage them. When you have the conversation during a non-stressful time and ask questions to gain information, you prepare for the future when the topic may evoke more emotion. Begin to research and record medication management options. With awareness, you may notice that medications have been missed or you have seen pills on the floor. You will recognize when the current strategy to manage medications may not be working due to memory or vision challenges. When you have a few ideas of a system that may work better, you can work together with your parent to adjust their behaviors and habits so that they can safely manage the process for as long as possible.

Driving

On his way to a full recovery after the stroke, Dad insisted he could still drive but turned over his keys and agreed to stop. Rather than stop, he continued to drive using his hidden stash of spare keys. I was battle-weary from our conflicts, and I was in the rapids, struggling to keep my head above water. There are sometimes clear signs that our parent should no longer be behind the wheel. Frequent fender benders, unexplained dents in the car, getting lost on familiar routes, and slow reactions are a few of the warning signs. If you have asked yourself the question or just wondered how you would know when it is time to have the conversation, then it is the right time to plan for the inevitability that your parent won't be able to drive at some point in the future. Prepare by researching and recording the alternative transportation options in the area. What activities are important for your parent to continue and what are the transportation options for each outing? This may not be the time to share your research. Rather, it is an exercise to help you prepare not only for the impact that this transition will have on your parent but also on you. Also, research the options for driving skills testing and an older adult driver's safety course. Have a conversation with the primary care physician or eye doctor to determine if they will be an ally when a conversation is imminent. Ride with your parent on occasion and assess safety. Check their vehicle for dents. If they have stopped going to destinations that involve a long or complicated route, would they consider trying one of the transportation options for those trips? Awareness will help you determine when to start the series of often emotionally charged conversations.

Getting Additional Help

The next time you are visiting your parents, make a mental note of housekeeping standards, and if all looks like business as usual, this can become your baseline. It may be a red flag if you start to see standards slipping. Is home maintenance up to date? Are there any pills on the floor where medicines are typically taken? Check the food in the refrigerator. Is it the quality and quantity that you would expect? Is there expired food? Do you have concerns about hygiene? If your parents have expressed a desire to age in place and you are helping here and there, consider how the situation will be managed when more help is required. Who will provide the support? Rather than take on more responsibility, research home care agencies and consider community services assistance such as grocery delivery. Begin to create a plan so that you can balance your needs and your life with care responsibilities. Awareness of your increased stress is a sign that your caregiver river has shifted, and that balance and boundaries may need to be revised.

Conversations and Planning

Plan a time to begin the discussions that will set your course. Decide the best day and time of day based on what you know about your parent's patterns and moods. For example, are your parents more conversational in the morning, afternoon, or evening? Is the weekend atmosphere calmer and a better time to have a conversation rather than active weekdays? What events trigger negative emotions and mood? You might coordinate the conversation to take place following an event that sparks a happy, more relaxed mood. Are your folks more receptive to a particular sibling? Let that sibling lead the discussion. Are you yourself an aging parent? If so, start planning the conversation with your adult kids. The plan you develop can be the talking points for discussing the topic with your parent(s). Another timing consideration is that the holidays are not the best time to have an in-depth conversation but are a good time to be aware, be realistic and begin to think about how to best prepare yourself and your older adults for what is around the next corner.

While you may not have a crystal ball, you have awareness and instinct. You can identify resources, ask questions, plan, and prepare for the transitions that appear on the horizon. Then, read the river to navigate the transitions with confidence.

8 HAVE THE CONVERSATIONS: BUILD YOUR BOAT TOGETHER

A person's success in life can usually be measured by the number of uncomfortable conversations he or she is willing to have.

TIMOTHY FERRISS,
THE 4-HOUR WORKWEEK

IN THE BEGINNING, conversations with Dad about legal and financial matters went well. He appreciated the help when I accompanied him on doctor's visits and took over billpaying duties. We visited his lawyer and established me as the primary power of attorney for health and business purposes. Since we often avoid these conversations until our options are limited, it was fortunate that we had the essential discussions before Dad's stroke. Our culture does not embrace aging, losing independence, and death as just another part of life. Sadly, we embrace fear and denial as we push these realities away. Agingcare.com shared noteworthy insight stating, "In America, going grey is regarded in a distinctly negative light." Michelle Barnhart, associate professor at Oregon State University clarified, "We go from thinking of ourselves as children, then young adults, then adults, then we stop."[40]

The foundation you develop through dialogue and mutual understanding will build a sustainable watercraft that will not only carry you confidently through the caregiving rapids but will also allow you to enjoy the serenity of the calm waters while you navigate your caregiving journey. How to have these conversations about the future is arguably more important than what to say during the discussions. It is critical to plan and be clear on your objectives before beginning. Set an intention. Understand that the goal is to keep the channels of communication open. Each discussion will not be a one-and-done conversation. Getting to win - win requires that you maximize empathy and minimize ego. Demonstrate vulnerability, compassion, and be curious.

When you begin a conversation with curiosity and a desire to understand your parent's situation and preferences, you demonstrate respect and set the tone for collaboration. When you practice active listening skills, you will more likely be heard later when you provide input. Active listening includes staying engaged without judgment or interruption. It involves repeating or paraphrasing what you heard and asking clarifying questions to better

---

[40] Anne-Marie Botek, "Why Seniors Refuse Help," *Aging Care,* accessed March 17 2021, https://www.agingcare.com/articles/old-people-refuse-help-154617.htm

understand rather than immediately jumping in with an opinion. Sensitive topics can arouse a defensive stance, and when it is clear that you are keeping an open mind, the dialogue will flow more freely. Keep in mind that you have not been their age nor faced the tough decisions that come with aging. Your relationship and role are changing. It may be helpful to look at your new relationship with your parent(s) as an alliance where you are working together as they begin to rely more on you, societal systems, and strategies to remain as independent as possible. It is important to remember that you are not reversing roles.

The conversations critical to sustainable caregiving include several sensitive subjects, and the strategy is similar for each of them. The strategy that I found to be the most effective incorporated patience and respect. I introduced a topic by asking a question, listened, and responded by demonstrating support and understanding. I often asked a follow-up question that planted a seed and then left the topic behind altogether. Most often, Dad brought the subject up within a few days. He would say that he had been thinking or he wanted my opinion on what we had discussed. I proceeded gently. The objective was to keep the lines of communication open rather than immediately reach a result or decision. By working together to arrive at a solution, we both understood the advantages and were invested in the outcome's success.

One of the first times that this strategy worked well was when Dad missed a few payments resulting in the cancellation of his home insurance. I asked questions about what might have happened, and while he didn't know, Dad was adamant that he did not miss a payment. Without disagreeing, I told him that I would take care of finding another insurance company and keep him in the loop. A few days later, he asked me to read a letter that arrived. It was a bill. He was concerned about missing something again and wanted to make sure he understood the details. Macular degeneration and glaucoma had wreaked havoc with his vision, so I wondered if maybe he hadn't been able to see or read previous bills clearly. I took this opportunity to ask if maybe that was what happened with the home insurance bill. He became defensive, and I let the subject go for the moment. Managing the mail and paying bills was not a responsibility that he was ready to relinquish but was something that I wanted to oversee a bit more closely until he was ready to accept more help.

Dad agreed to add me to his bank account, and in the spirit of collaboration, I ordered large print checks designed for persons with low visibility so that he could continue to pay bills. With Dad's approval, I set up a few auto payments. Soon after, Dad missed a life insurance payment when he mistakenly threw away the payment notice. He acknowledged that he threw it out because the payments were most often automatically paid with dividends. He was still defensive about his role in the mishap. Without judgment, I offered to review the mail before it was tossed, and he agreed. Also, when I handed him the mail and saw a bill, I offered to pay it. Trust was established. I was helping rather than taking over these responsibilities. The combination of small respectful conversations and micro-steps of collaboration ultimately led to Dad letting me manage all the mail and bills.

The most important place to start regarding financial matters is to know where financial documents are kept. You might start the conversation by asking a few questions such as, "Do you have a financial advisor? What plans have been made that you can share? Could we set up a meeting so that I may meet your advisor?" Other vital questions include, "Where do you bank? What insurance policies do you have? Where are the documents and the contact information for banks, brokers, and insurance information kept?"

The next step may be monitoring accounts. Your concern might be that your parents are vulnerable to fraud, and it is a valid concern. Older adults can be a bit too trusting, lonely, polite, and financially well established, making them prime targets for fraud. The tactics used by the fraudster are well-honed and may involve months of trust and relationship development. At some point, more oversight will be needed. Begin the conversations, and don't be discouraged by rejection. Occasionally, revisit the subject with empathy and openness.

Another subject that will require thoughtful conversations is legal matters regarding health. If a health care representative has not been designated, it is an essential first step to ensure that your parents' decisions are upheld if they cannot share their preferences. The Five

Wishes[41] booklet is a great place to begin documenting your parent's choices and can help initiate meaningful dialogue. With witness signatures, the document is valid in 42 states. Other circumstances and needs may be better suited to an attorney. Elder law attorneys specialize in a variety of elder law issues. It is best to locate an attorney whose focus matches your situation. The National Academy of Elder Law Attorneys, https://www.naela.org, offers a directory and information on the advantages of selecting an attorney who regularly manages your particular concerns. As with all professional services, referrals and recommendations are an excellent place to start. Attorney fees are handled in various ways, and it is important to understand the payment details before committing to a collaboration.

A few questions to get the conversation started include, "Do you have a Durable POA or a Health Care POA? Do you have an attorney? If so, is she familiar with elder law issues and may I meet your attorney? If not, what do you think about finding an attorney? Do you have a living will? Where are your legal documents stored?" These questions lead to more questions. When you are designated as an attorney-in-fact on a POA for your parent, it is crucial to know their wishes and understand their health status so that you may be their advocate either making sure their stated wishes are followed or making decisions for them on issues not addressed in a POA. A hospitalization or disease diagnosis can be the first time many family members know a parent's medical details. Suddenly, there is a lot to learn

---

41   Five Wishes, accessed September 7, 2019, https://fivewishes.org

and with a rapidity that is ripe for errors. Receiving an introduction to your parent's current health and medical condition before a crisis will reduce the learning curve. This knowledge will help you participate more confidently, formulate questions, and collaborate on decisions to advocate for your parent.

Fortunately, I went to doctor's appointments with Dad and was aware of his medical history. I made spreadsheets with some of the details, such as medications and hospitalizations. He was grateful that I could answer the frequently asked questions and appreciative that I asked the questions he and I had discussed before the appointment. He often had his own written list of questions. When I asked a question, I phrased it in a way that included Dad as the questioner. When we were asked a question, I let Dad answer first. I could tell by Dad's expression when he misunderstood or didn't hear what was asked and often had to repeat the question. When I did add input, it was respectful, often answering to Dad so that the doctor would hear, and Dad didn't feel like he was excluded. For example, if the doctor asked if Dad had any trouble walking and Dad replied, "No." I would say, "Dad, remember how you were telling me that you felt off balance when you went for a walk or when you were walking to and from the kitchen?" It helped us change the course of the conversation and focus on solutions. It allowed Dad to view me as someone in his corner rather than someone "telling on him." It ensured that our conversations at home remained open and that

Dad continued to share his challenges with me so that I could be an effective care partner.

Learn about your parent's health and begin to develop relationships with the professionals in your parent's circles. Questions to initiate the discussion around health include, "How do you like your primary care physician? May I meet them? Who are your other key doctors? What is your relationship like with them? How do you manage your medications? Do you keep a medications list? May I have a copy? Have you thought about alternative ways to manage medications like ordering them pre-sorted or having them delivered? What do you think about starting a health care journal to document visit details?"

You could share a story of a friend who went through hospitalization or an article you read that will help lead to more questions. You may have thought about some of these questions as they relate to your situation and could lead with your vulnerabilities. For example, "I was just reading about the percentage of hospitalizations that result in a return to the hospital within weeks of discharge. There were some tips to prevent it from happening. Have you ever thought about how a trip to the hospital might change things at home? It makes me think about how it is so important to maintain good health. How are you staying fit and eating healthy?" You get the idea. The conversation may be fact-finding and seed planting but can still be conversational.

Another vital factor in well-being is social interaction and satisfaction. You might ask. "Are you happy with the amount of time you spend with friends, on hobbies and interests?" Understanding if your parent is lonely, feels isolated, or bored will allow you to help them participate or expand their interests. Helping them stay engaged and healthy will keep their living arrangement options open and, in turn, keep your options open. You are a team.

Where your parent lives will impact you as well. For years, a friend assumed that she would move in with her mom when her mom began to need more assistance. Her siblings assumed the same thing, but there had never been a conversation with their mom. Recently, her mom said that that was never going to happen. It was a wake-up call. My friend's mom was going through treatments and had significant health considerations. The conversation was overdue. Another friend received a call from her mom. Mom said, "Your dad and I want to know if you want us to put a deposit on a retirement home here in Florida or closer to you in Tennessee?" That simple question sparked many talking points and opened communication channels for a more in-depth discussion.

You could start your conversation by asking, "Where would you like to be in 10, 20, 30 years? What would be your ideal living situation in X years? Is that possible financially?" You could also bring attention to challenges in the home. You can ask, "Those steps may get tricky if your knee keeps acting up. Have you thought about creating age-friendly spaces or downsizing?" You can also begin to discuss what your role will look like in the future, "How do you imagine we (family) will be involved down the road?"

Dad wasn't very receptive to the "What if" questions that I presented. He considered them to be negative thinking. If I had asked the questions sooner, before many of the outcomes were imminent, we might have had a better back and forth about the realities of aging. It is not fun to talk about the worst that could happen, but it is comforting to be prepared with the knowledge of your parent's preferences. Ask yourself, "What is the worst that could happen? What is the best possible outcome?" Discuss what options are possibilities for each of these outcomes.

Aging in place takes planning, coordination, and cooperation. If that is your parent's choice, it may be helpful to set the stage. I wanted Dad to remain independent and took over more and more responsibilities to facilitate his independence. His reality became an illusion of autonomy. Our arrangement worked well until I was doing more than I could manage without negatively impacting my well-being. When I suggested that we hire someone to help, Dad asserted that he was doing just fine on his own and didn't need help. I took a step back and used the conversation strategy that had worked well previously. I planted a seed by sharing that I was having trouble managing the work to keep things going around the house. I shared that I needed help. I asked him if he would mind if occasionally, I had someone else give him a ride to the wellness center, church, or to get his groceries. I let the questions sit for a few days. He agreed, and we added a few folks to the care team. These team members were not well received at first, but when Dad appreciated the aides as new friends who would take him on outings, listen to his stories and share a bit about their families, he warmed to the idea of accepting help. I also received the support I needed to continue to provide care while also focusing on my well-being.

It would have been better to have set the scene in advance by asking a few questions such as, "What will it look like when I begin to help out more and more? Have you considered what it might be like to have someone helping with chores? What type of person would help the most – someone chatty or quiet? Someone who enjoys history? Someone who can cook? What would be the ideal schedule?"

There were other ways to receive help. Dad was not a fan of delivered meals because he delivered meals in his younger days, and it made him feel old to have them delivered to him. And, from his recollection, they did not taste good. It did not matter that there were new services with tasty meals. It was the principle that he resisted. Before I took over managing the meals, a conversation could have changed his sensitivity. For example, "There are many new meal service agencies. Have you tried any of them? Would you like to look at grocery delivery? Some agencies offer help with housekeeping and meals. Are you familiar with any in the area?" As driving and transportation became a challenge, I might have shared, "There are several alternatives to driving. We use Uber and Lyft occasionally. Would you be interested in trying any of the ride options for more extended or nighttime drives?"

Dad was open to discussing a move to an independent living facility, and we toured a few. We even put deposits down, but Dad decided after further consideration that he was not interested in moving. He made his wishes clear and was going to remain in his place. Hence, we shifted our focus to creating the optimum environment for all of us, which meant shared inconvenience, but overall workability. Behind the scenes, I made plans for his worst-case scenario and knew what we would do if an event led to Dad moving to a care facility. I could see why Dad wanted to stay in his home. At first glance, the independent living facilities seemed like resorts. The pools, activities, meals, and social scene seemed ideal. The resort view was through my eyes. When I looked at the residence through Dad's eyes, I saw the facility that he saw and understood his fear of moving. Dad was in his 90's and a conversation a decade earlier may have begun with, "How was the decision made for your mom to move in with you and Mom? What did Grandma think about the arrangement? How did the transition go? What was the most challenging aspect of living together? Have you thought about where you want to live when you need more help? What are your thoughts on living in a retirement community? Have you visited a friend who lives in any of the communities nearby? Are there any that you would like to visit and tour?"

Keep curiosity and respect at the forefront of the conversations. Revisit topics at opportunistic times, such as when a friend has a relevant experience, or a subject arises in the news that sparks further dialogue. Together, begin to build a vision of the future that includes various scenarios. At the same time, anticipate that desires may change as reality approaches. Remain flexible and prioritize collaboration.

Sustainability includes finding meaning and purpose in our journey. Simply helping our parent is purposeful, yet we want them to thrive. Conversations focused on legacy can be some of the most memorable and meaningful interactions that you have with your parents and these conversations will add value to their aging experience. Legacy is more than leaving a gift of money or property, a plaque, or a great act of benevolence. It wasn't until I read David Solie's book, *How to Say it to Seniors: Closing the Communication Gap with Our Elders*[42], that I understood the importance of legacy. Processing our life stories is a developmental task that becomes increasingly important when we review our lives and question how we will be remembered. Our legacy is the meaning of our acts and how they are connected to our values. This knowledge helped me understand many of Dad's requests and repeated stories. It helped me understand why he fixated on certain parts of his life and exhibited minimal regard for others. It helped me help him make

---

42 David Solie, *How to Say it to Seniors: Closing the Communication Gap with Our Elders*, (Prentice Hall Press, 2004) Kindle edition

meaning of those periods of his life by asking questions and sharing my impressions of his stories.

David Solie tells us that, "Whether they express it or not, life review is the dominant psychological event of getting old.... Senior adults focus on reviewing their lives to find what it meant for them to have lived." He clarifies that this is the primary concern, after control over their present and future. An essential part of our role is to help our parents process their life stories in a way that allows them to discover the meaning that will continue when they are no longer here. We can only fulfill this important task if we are not in a battle for control over legal, financial, or independence matters. Listening to your parent during critical conversations is a gift to both you and them.

To help your parents process their life story:

1. Look for clues and opportunities such as a story that is shared repeatedly.
2. Listen for new detail and explore the meaning.
3. Focus on values or themes.
4. Ask open ended, clarifying questions.
5. Allow pauses without jumping in to speak.
6. Summarize or repeat what you heard and then relate it to something in your own experience to help them further process and explore the meaning.

To initiate a conversation on legacy, you could begin with the powerful prompt, "Tell me about…" You could explore passions and interests such as music, movies, travel, sports, and hobbies. Learn the back story of photographs and memorabilia. The book, *300 Questions to Ask Your Parents Before It's Too Late,* by Shannon Alder[43] is a fantastic tool to get the conversation ball rolling. You might ask them to document their life story and the events that shaped who they are. The stories and lessons could be captured and shared in any combination of writing, photos, video, or voice. This record will become an amazing gift.

These conversations are good practice for one of the most important conversations you will have with your parents. Once you understand how your parents want to live, you will want to understand how they want to die. Discussing end-of-life is not comfortable, and our society does not prepare us well for conversations about death. It is a part of life, but like aging, death is often not faced until there's a forced confrontation. This discussion is much less emotionally charged when end-of-life is not imminent. With a bit of preparation, you will feel empowered and proud of yourself for initiating a conversation that has probably already been on your parent's mind.

When we approach this conversation by demonstrating our own vulnerability, we create a safe space for family members to express their feelings and emotions.

---

[43] Shannon Alder, *300 Questions to Ask Your Parents Before It's Too Late,* (Horizon Publishers, 2011)

Being vulnerable takes courage. Having these conversations takes courage. Acknowledge that the subject is unsettling and uncomfortable to discuss. Sit with the discomfort and then lean into it. Explore your fears. Curiosity about your own thoughts surrounding end-of-life will help you begin the conversation with your parents. When we are curious and seek to understand, we avoid assumptions. You may be surprised to find that your reflection on death brought you to an entirely different place than that of your parent. The most important outcome, especially in the early discussions, is to keep communication lines open.

Prepare for the discussion by learning end-of-life terms, concepts, and components. With this knowledge, you can decide the order and depth of what you want to discuss as you progress. Advance directives are a good place to start because of the significance of understanding your family member's wishes before any incapacitation might set in and then designating a person who will support and communicate those wishes if required. The terms below are a starting point for learning. Specific terms can vary from state to state.

- Advance directives are the documents that indicate one's wishes should they not be able to communicate them independently. They include a living will and a POA for health care.[44]

---

[44] "Advance directive vs. living will: What's the difference?" FreeWill.com, Last updated: August 5, 2021
https://www.freewill.com/learn/advance-directive-vs-living-will

- A living will is a health care declaration. It includes a statement of desired medical treatment.
- A Healthcare POA or Medical POA designates a proxy to make medical decisions in case of incapacity and to communicate with the patient's doctor to ensure treatment wishes are honored.
- A do not resuscitate order, DNR, is a statement declining CPR if the patient's heart stops beating. It is an order arranged and signed before an emergency.
- Physician Orders for Life-Sustaining Treatment, POLST, is a form that communicates treatment wishes. A POLST is used in addition to a Medical POA.[45]

Other end-of-life topics for discussion include cemetery and funeral arrangements. You might start by asking, "Have you made funeral and burial plans?" End-of-life conversations with Dad had taken place over the years. In the beginning, it was helpful to gain clarity on his vision for a good death. It helped guide future discussions. The peace of mind was a significant gift to us both. Dad shared that he wanted to be buried, not cremated, but was unwilling to discuss funeral arrangements. He was adamant that this was the responsibility of the family to manage after death. It was a firmly held generational viewpoint, and I decided that continuing to broach the

---

45   Robert Sawicki, "Difference Between Power of Attorney & POLST," *OSF Healthcare* blog, September 17, 2013, https://www.osfhealthcare.org/blog/difference-between-power-of-attorney-polst/

subject was more harmful than helpful. In hindsight, if I had started the conversations a decade earlier, the outcome may have been more productive.

It is essential to understand how and where your family member wants to spend their final days. It is helpful to understand the types of care available when a serious illness has been diagnosed. Gain a better understanding of palliative care and end-of-life doula services. Researching these resources will provide information that may help guide your conversation. It is not uncommon to begin the conversation and be met with resistance. When met with a refusal to continue the discussion, table it, and revisit the subject later. You may make a small amount of headway during each attempt until you achieve a breakthrough. It is worth the effort to continue because when you know your parent's wishes, you can help them achieve their vision.

When Dad was diagnosed with interstitial lung disease, he qualified for hospice services. The conversation that led us to accept these services was sensitive. Dad agreed to go into hospice care because together we were concerned about the risks involved with even basic care during the COVID-19 pandemic. We discussed that we could stop hospice care when the concern was alleviated. The benefits were many. Medicines linked to the diagnosis were covered by Medicare and distributed by the hospice pharmacy. We had access to a nurse and physician 24/7. A nurse visited bi-weekly. Weekly visits were also an option. A social worker was available if we needed emotional support as well as a non-denominational clergy member. If required, the care team included aides to help Dad with bathing and other daily activities. In addition, volunteers were available to sit with Dad. Due to COVID-19, we declined many of the services available, but we appreciated the round-the-clock access to a nurse and doctor if needed.

Begin your research with agencies that offer palliative care, hospice organizations, and end-of-life doulas. A palliative care team consists of doctors, nurses, social workers, chaplains, and nutritionists. The team works with the family and the patient to support medical, emotional, comfort, and practical needs. Care can be provided at home or in a facility. Medicare, Medicaid, the U.S. Department of Veterans Affairs, and some private insurance companies may cover palliative care, but not always. The main difference between palliative care and hospice care is that patients may continue to receive lifesaving treatments under palliative care.

Like palliative care, hospice services also consist of a similar team of professionals, and the support goals are the same. Medicare pays for hospice care. When accepted due to a qualifying disease, you agree to stop lifesaving procedures. The focus is on comfort and quality of life. An end-of-life doula or death doula helps the patient and family navigate the end-of-life process. A doula can spend more time with the patient and attends to a deeper level of emotional support. They provide families with information that helps them prepare for the transition, including guiding family members through the final conversations crucial for closure. The doula can help the family personalize the transition for the patient. The International End of Life Doula Association has a Doula Directory that could be helpful. General research into palliative care, hospice care, and end-of-life doula services may lead to specific resources. It would be valuable to establish relationships with individuals or organizations. You may also want to receive materials to file for future reference or ask questions about concerns.

Each conversation will be a building block that will lead to future meaningful discussions. These discussions will enable you to create and continue to develop the plan that will give you peace of mind, which is at the core of sustainable caregiving.

9 HOSPITALIZATIONS HAPPEN - HAVE A PLAN: MULTI-DAY SIDE TRIP ITINERARY

Learn from the mistakes of others. You can't live long enough to make them all yourself.

ADMIRAL HYMAN G. RICKOVER, *ADDRESS TO THE CALIFORNIA DEMOCRATIC COUNCIL*

WHILE CARING FOR a family member is an expedition, a hospital stay can be a shorter, whirlwind side-trip. A hospitalization may be planned in the case of elective surgery, or it may be unexpected. Either way, it can be an exhausting, stressful experience for the family caregiver. Any hospitalization is a significant event that can be the start of the caregiver's decline into burnout if not managed in a way that creates a sustainable post hospital situation. Sustainability begins before admission. Specific strategies and preparedness will help lessen the stress and keep the caregiver from going adrift into dangerous waters.

Before a hospital admission

Pre-planning for a known or unexpected hospitalization will allow you to focus on your family member and their care with confidence. Document your family member's medical history, including doctor's visits, medication changes and results, as well as symptoms. Keep a log of physicians' contact information. Research and collect disease-specific information that will help you understand the progression. Note the national and local support resources that are available.

When you have the Healthcare POA in place prior to a hospitalization and know your family member's wishes, you eliminate the stress of trying to accomplish this task when managing a crisis. Next, create and coordinate a patient advocate team, if possible. The patient advocate is a demanding role when fulfilled solely by the primary caregiver. Ideally, someone would be at the bedside during all hours possible to communicate with the doctors, specialists and primary care physician, nurses, and techs. Who in your circle of friends and family can help you? It is crucial to learn and understand changes in prescribed medicines and treatments. What tests are being performed, why, and what are the results? Having someone present facilitates accurate communication in both directions, from the patient to the staff and staff to the patient. It is challenging during the best of times to hear, understand and convey medical information and increasingly more complicated in a hospital setting.

During a hospitalization

Strategize for your well-being and self-care during and after the hospital stay. How might a modified routine help you get adequate sleep and nutrition when you spend all your free time at the hospital? Opportunities to eat will be unpredictable and grazing will be easier and more successful than trying to eat three regular meals. Protein is a key ingredient that will help you stay sharp and feel full. What snacks can you keep on hand and in your vehicle or bag that will give you the energy and nutrients that will sustain you? Consider carrying a small cooler with hard boiled eggs, Greek yogurt, hummus and vegetables, cottage cheese, a meat snack or plant-based meat. Nuts and protein bars are also good options. It is tempting to run through a drive-through on your way home in the evening and while you definitely deserve comfort food, you will be better served by stocking quick healthy options such as a salad, wrap or sandwich fixings.

Who can step in and be your parent's advocate so that you may take breaks? How will you spend your breaks? What are your most pressing needs? What will help bring you back to center and ground you: sleep, exercise, quiet time? During these breaks you might consider how care responsibilities will change when your loved one returns home. Consider your boundaries and begin to make plans to protect the hobbies and interests that keep you feeling healthy and whole. Will more of your time be required to provide care for your family member? Will the duties exceed your level of comfort? Continue to learn about illnesses and research disease progression that may impact the future. Family members may fill in the care gaps or you may need to enlist the help of paid caregivers. Begin to research home care agencies in the area. Read reviews. Ask for referrals. What other agencies can provide support? Will there be transportation needs? Contact the local Area Agency on Aging to identify local care and transportation resources. Make a plan A, B, and C when possible.

Record and track medication changes or concerning behaviors. The record will provide a means to look back at events, symptoms, or patterns. Recording details can help you stay organized and more efficiently manage care. You won't need to rely on memory which can be unreliable under stress. When a health care professional asks for medical history, you will be prepared and confident as your family member's advocate.

Prepare for discharge
Talk to the case manager or social worker and request resources to help you with support after discharge. Ask questions and gather information so that when your family member is back in your care, you are prepared to fulfill any responsibilities that were performed by the hospital staff and will need to continue at home. Write questions down as they come to you so that you are not relying on memory when you have a few moments with a specialist. What do you need to learn so that you can handle new procedures? Consider taking a video of any

process that will become your responsibility such as transfers (e.g., moving from bed to chair) or wound care. What permanent medication changes will carry over after discharge, and do you have those prescriptions? Will you be responsible for managing symptoms and what do you need to know? What mobility aids will be needed? Who should you call if you have a care question after returning home? When is the next appointment with the doctor? If rehab is a planned step before returning home and you will be able to choose the facility, begin to research the options. Ask your PCP for a recommendation. If you have time, visit a few locations. Begin to have conversations with the home care agencies that you researched.

Is the home a safe environment or will adjustments be required? An occupational therapist will likely do an assessment and offer recommendations, but a review of hazards may be helpful. Stairs, throw rugs and slippery shower floors can be dangerous.

At home
Make a list of help that might be needed such as meals, errands and grocery delivery, transportation, lawn maintenance, housekeeping, companion and sitting services. Determine the person or other resource that is the best fit for each need and begin to make the requests. When someone offers help, be prepared with ways they can participate. If needs exceed family and friend resources, an agency or private aid may be the solution.

If home health care has been prescribed, therapists such as a physical therapist and occupational therapist along with a nurse will visit providing an opportunity for more training. If you will be assisting with bathing, dressing, and toileting, these professionals can offer methods to keep you and your family member as safe and comfortable as possible.

My hospitalization side trips

See if my journey resonates with you. What would you have done differently? Dad spent a lot of time at the hospital but at 94, he had never spent a night in a hospital. He volunteered, drove staff and patients from the entrance to their vehicles in a large golf cart, where he felt right at home. From ages 94 to 97, however, he experienced the hospital on three occasions as a patient. Dad's first hospitalization soon followed the addition of blood thinner to his prescribed medicines. He had complained of an irregular heartbeat off and on for years. Each time, it was recommended that he wear a heart rate monitor, and each time he refused. Then, he relented and, a few days into the process, refused again. I was furious. He gave in long enough that the irregular heartbeats could be recorded, and an atrial fibrillation (A-Fib) diagnosis made. He went on the blood thinner Coumadin. It was a high-maintenance medication. He was covered in bruises. We had to have his blood INR (international normalized ratio) checked weekly. This test measured the time it took for his blood to clot so that the dosage could be adjusted accordingly. When the correct dosage was determined, the frequency of testing would be reduced to every two to four weeks. We could not get the dosing just right and the weekly tests continued for months. I was sliding down a slippery slope, focused on following the rules and consumed with worry. Head down, I didn't do research and so I was not aware of the alternatives to Coumadin. I lacked perspective and as the intensity increased, I allowed circumstances and Dad's behavior to wreak havoc with my peace of mind.

Weeks after the A-Fib diagnosis, he had an intestinal bleed in the middle of the night and was taken to the hospital where I spent every waking hour. This was something I could do, I wanted to do, and Dad needed me. It was not the best decision for my well-being, and it was not sustainable. It was the beginning of poor choices that did not facilitate a balance between my well-being and Dad's health and comfort. I had been around hospitals. Mom had rheumatic fever when she was three. Her heart had been damaged, and because of the damage, she had three heart surgeries, one before she got married, one when I was seven, and one when I was in my 30's. Other related complications caused her to spend time in many hospitals. Lessons I learned early were that mistakes would happen during a hospitalization, misunderstandings were inevitable, and mishaps were sure to occur at home following a hospitalization. It would be wonderful if we could learn everything we needed to know from the mistakes of others. There were so many complexities involved in each hospital stay that the best I could do was know that mistakes, misunderstandings, and mishaps were inescapable. I could plan accordingly and let compassion direct my response.

When I accepted this inevitability, I was better prepared for the role of Dad's advocate. Acceptance, compassion, and forgiveness were three strategies that I relied on as I advocated for Dad by:

- Writing down information as it was explained and asking questions to clarify the confusing bits
- Jotting down the questions that surfaced in the middle of the night
- Demonstrating self-compassion when I didn't live up to absurdly high standards
- Recording procedures that I needed to replicate at home and to imagine performing these tasks to identify potential complications
- Learning as much as possible about diagnosis, recovery, or ramifications
- Paying attention and engaging with the care team
- Showing appreciation for all that was being done for my family member while many others are also receiving care
- Talking to the discharge planner about medications and care needed at home

Dad's second hospitalization was the result of stopping the blood thinner that caused the first hospitalization. We decided that Coumadin wasn't worth the risk, and after collaborating with the doctor, Dad stopped taking it. Weeks later, he had a stroke. It had happened sometime in the night, and I drove him to the ER in the morning. It was a busy place. They did not have a bed, so they kept wheeling him back behind the locked doors for tests. For several reasons, I should have called 911 rather than driven him myself. If he had been taken by ambulance, assessment and possible treatment would have begun in the ambulance. He would have been receiving medical attention and under the care of medical professionals immediately rather than riding in the car and sitting in the waiting room. If anyone is counting the mistakes, I had made four sizable ones to this point, but if I had not insisted on him continuing to wear the heart monitor, we would have been right where we were at this moment, in the ER.

Dad spent a week in the hospital. I was there again each day, from morning until night. The neurologist stopped coming by after a few days. At the end of the stay, I was told that he stopped coming because Dad would make a full recovery. That would have been comforting information to have known at any moment earlier. Dad was still pointing at the blue and saying yellow and confusing simple images. He wasn't walking well, and his words weren't coming to him. The day Dad was discharged from the hospital to rehab, the social worker handed me a packet of information. Welcome to the deep end. At home that night, blurry eyed from lack of sleep, I went through each form and applied for everything available. More decisions. There were waiting lists, and I put Dad on all of them. I had no idea what we would need when he recovered or what he would accept in the way of help. Why didn't any of those forms have the name of someone who had been through this, someone who could relate to the turmoil, someone who could tell me that how I was feeling was normal and that it would be alright?

I chose a rehab facility that was also a hospital. It was a trek to visit every day, but I preferred that the therapy match Dad's motivation, and I believed that this was the best option. In a week, he was almost back to "his normal" and was demanding to leave. I would have preferred that he remain in the rehab facility for the recommended two weeks, but as his advocate and armed with the knowledge of our options at home, I began the process to request an exception and have him released after one week. The responsibility of making these decisions weighed heavily on me and the uncertainty of whether I made the best choice, the right decision, was a constant worry. It was a lonely space.

The question of where Dad would go following rehab came up repeatedly. While he was always going to return to his home, I learned that there were two clear camps. People in camp 1 were incredulous when they thought I would consider sending Dad to an assisted living facility. People in camp 2 told me I would not survive otherwise. The PT at the rehab hospital told me that if I were a good daughter, I would take care of him at home. Later at home, the visiting PT and OT told me that providing care at home was not sustainable, that I would burn out. They gave me personal examples. It was all too sudden, and I had no idea how to know what was suitable or sustainable. After some maneuvering, I sprung him from rehab, and he continued physical therapy and occupational therapy at home.

One thing was clear. I needed help with the tasks that swirled around Dad's care. There were doctor's appointments, cooking, cleaning, laundry, Veterans Affairs forms, medication management, physical therapy, occupational therapy, and in-home nurses to coordinate, grocery shopping, gear shopping (walker, cane, portable toilet), installation of safety bars, and implementation of low vision recommendations. In addition, it took time and effort to keep Dad engaged in current events and stocked in painting supplies, badger him to do physical therapy exercises, update friends and family members on his progress, plus a host of other activities needed to keep him going. I learned that "It takes a village" did not just apply to raising children. I also learned that the "help that helped" changed with the intensity of the experience, and I needed to regroup, reassess and re-source when I struggled.

I was overwhelmed and was infuriated that Dad insisted that he didn't need help. Insisting that he could still drive, he refused to give me the key that he remembered he had found tucked away (not the last of the hidden keys). It felt like Dad resisted my every move to create a safe living space and manage his medicines. He wanted the bedside commode out of the house and into the dumpster. Dad did not want help, did not need help, and would not have help. He was getting along just fine. I, however, was losing my mind and told him that I needed help. Boundaries are ours to set, modify and reinforce. He reluctantly agreed. I found a home care company, and my learning continued. The aide would arrive, and Dad would say, "I really don't know why you're here. I don't need any help." I had to learn how to manage the entire situation, which created a lot of additional stress in the beginning. The reality was that I needed help beyond the tasks and resources. I needed help with the emotions, the resistance, the worries.

Dad's third significant hospitalization was planned. His partial knee replacement 21 years prior was no longer viable. X-rays revealed a shift in the components, and it was producing pain to the degree that he could no longer comfortably walk. He wanted the knee replaced and found the surgeon who would do it. Dad was 97, and after resisting the idea for many months, I relented and reluctantly supported his efforts. In hindsight, it was his decision to make, and my resistance may have caused his pain to prevent him from exercising, which would have enabled him to be stronger before surgery. Knowing when to acquiesce and accept Dad's decisions was something I struggled to learn. Acceptance required that I acknowledge when my fears were motivating my resistance. Dad was unwilling to live with the pain or lose his mobility, and he was willing to take the risk to live life on his terms or not live at all. Dad, with an understanding of the risks, was entitled to make his own decisions. The role that I had accepted as his caregiver was best carried out by supporting those decisions.

I wasn't concerned about him not surviving the surgery; it was the post-surgery period that worried me. Operation day, Dad did fine, and we chatted after the surgery. He was upbeat and sharp. I was tremendously relieved and went to get something to eat. While I was gone, the nurse gave Dad half of the prescribed pain medication because the full dose seemed high for his age. When I returned, I couldn't wake him. I had only been gone 20 minutes. I asked them to call Dad's primary care physician, who I knew was in the hospital. A nurse asked if I wanted them to administer Narcan to reverse all of the pain medicine. The question caused as much anxiety as the situation because I was not qualified to make that call, and the risks seemed tremendous. I made it clear that Dad's doctor was the one who needed to make that decision.

I became the patient advocate that Dad needed and made several other immediate requests and a few that were to stay in effect through the night including no more pain medication unless he requested it and if he did, I wanted to be notified. I requested a report of all the medicine in his system because I wanted to verify that he had not been given general anesthesia, which he had not. The pain medication he was given over the course of the day was more than enough to cause an overdose. The nurse saved his life when she didn't give him that full dose. Twenty-four hours later, with no new pain medicine, he was still so high that he couldn't answer correctly when asked his name. I learned that understanding what pain medication was prescribed post-surgery was equally, if not more important than questioning pre-surgery anesthesia and medication. It finally wore off. A 97-year-old in good health can survive the surgery, but the aftercare must consider age. It had been acknowledged by many of the team members that they did not have much experience with the recovery process for someone Dad's age. The doctor who performed the surgery told me to stop lecturing him; he had thousands of patients. Toe to toe, I said, "You may have had thousands of patients; I have one Dad."

When hospitalizations happen, be the advocate your family member needs by being prepared, being present, and being a partner in their care. Support yourself on this side trip so that you are strong enough to support the patient. Mistakes will happen, but compassion and forgiveness will help you remain focused on the objective, which is for your family member to be discharged and transition safely to the next step of care where your work continues.

10   TAKING THE WHEEL: ORIENT YOURSELF FOR THE TRANSITION

Life seems sometimes like nothing more than a series of losses, from beginning to end. That's the given. How you respond to those losses, what you make of what's left, that's the part you have to make up as you go.

KATHARINE WEBER,
THE MUSIC LESSON

THE DECISIONS SURROUNDING driving can result in some of the most emotionally charged conversations during the caregiving experience. While there are accounts of older adults voluntarily handing over the keys and declaring that they no longer feel safe driving, that is often not how the scenario unfolds. It is crucial to understand what is at stake for your family member and for you as a caregiver when driving is no longer an option. Your family member is losing the freedom and independence to manage his or her own life. This is likely one of several successive losses and can result in a grip onto the wheel that can look like a grip holding onto life itself. To navigate this transition in a way that sustains your relationships and emotional well-being, it is crucial to understand the loss from your family member's perspective so that you engage from a place of compassion and empathy. It is vital to begin with the end in mind and focus on common objectives to avoid the wounds of a potentially epic battle.

Imagine if, at this moment, you no longer had access to a vehicle nor the ability to use a ride share service. Would you feel anger, fear, panic? It can be challenging for us to empathize with our family member's loss when our own fear is based on the potential dangers each time our family member gets behind the wheel. Our impression of their abilities is entirely at odds with their impression of their own abilities. When Dad no longer had a valid driver's license due to poor vision, he insisted on continuing to drive and hid his car key. He was not unique in his pursuits, and his motivations made perfect sense considering his circumstances, the losses he had already experienced, and his vested interest in remaining independent. After months of intense conflict, the dust settled, but there were wounds and battle scars. My ego was the only winner at the end, which meant that there were no real winners.

Planning, preparing, and practicing awareness are the steps you can take now so that when the time is right for a transition, you will be able to support your family member through the actions that will help them maintain a sense of continued control and independence. Learn the signs that will alert you to a needed change. With awareness you can determine when to move forward. Planning will help your parent remain connected to the people and interests that fashion their identity and add quality to their lives. Preparing for both the conversations and the new methods of mobility will minimize stress.

Awareness

My awareness was skewed by denial. The tipping point was when a man followed Dad home and angrily insisted that he be more careful. Dad had run through a slew of ibises. Ibises are gentle white birds that feed in the grass and leisurely cross the road throughout the neighborhood. Dad claimed that they ran out in front of his car, and he couldn't avoid them. Likely, he never saw them and likely wasn't aware of the incident until the horrified witness brought him to task. My brother Pat shared another concerning account. It was nighttime, and Dad was in the lane to turn right at a red light. A pedestrian started into the street, and Dad proceeded forward. The pedestrian stopped. Pat alerted Dad, who also stopped. The pedestrian started. Dad started. Pat yelled. It was a loop. Dad never saw the pedestrian.

There had been other signs - scratches and dents. Dad and I were both in denial. We were both at risk of losing our freedom, so I avoided the conversation until it was painfully obvious that we needed to make a change. I was not prepared for this level of conflict. Nor had I planned the next steps that would have made the transition less traumatic.

To ease the transition, take a ride with your family member to evaluate reaction time, how increased traffic is handled, lane changing challenges, vision difficulty, or missed turns. Is driving speed significantly slower than the speed limit, or do you notice sudden or unnecessary braking? This ride is your baseline. Plan a regularly scheduled ride and note any changes. Check out the vehicle and look for scratches and dents. You may take photos or keep a log. Your parent may share a story about a concerning incident or a close call, but the details may be fuzzy. These are all clues that indicate that a change is on the horizon and preparations are in order.

After a few ride-alongs, identify the specific concerns you have about your family member's driving abilities. You may be particularly focused on vision, hearing, reaction time, cognitive issues, or have concerns about a medical condition. For example, if eyesight is the challenge, understand the DMV guidelines in your state to qualify for a license and plan to attend your family member's next eye exam. Have a conversation with the tech or doctor before the visit and share your concern. If reaction time is the concern, a driving test designed for elderly drivers may be warranted for peace of mind. Check with the local DMV, AARP, or AAA Club locations for information and resources. Is memory a concern? Has your parent gotten lost on a familiar route? You might research a neurologist who specializes in age-related cognitive issues and begin testing for dementia. An early diagnosis increases options. If a medical condition or prescribed medication is a concern, discuss the worry with the doctor. When you have a worry, make a plan. The plan will help you from obsessing over the worry. It will also help you take action when the time is right rather than getting caught up in stressful research.

Be prepared with choices so that you can collaborate to create a plan. Self-driving cars may be the solution of the future. Until then, identify the senior and disability transportation options in the community. Start with the local Area Agency on Aging. Research the public transportation services to identify the systems in place for senior transit. Learn about eligibility requirements. Request forms and information. Is there a waiting list? What is the cost per ride, and how is payment handled? What mobility challenges will need to be considered? How complicated is it to schedule a ride? Does the schedule look adequate to accommodate needs, and are there distance or other limitations such as the number of eligible passengers per vehicle?

Planning & Preparation
Once you understand the options and have more information about what may lead to a transition away from driving, you can begin to prepare by focusing on the details. List the places that your family member goes and begin to consider and match each outing's transportation

options. Consider how scheduled appointments versus hobbies or interests may be managed. Research services that may reduce trips, such as prescription delivery, grocery delivery, meal service plans or Amazon Pantry. If shopping is also an opportunity for exercise and entertainment, how can that continue to be a part of the activities? Where will you or your family and friends fill in the gaps?

You can choose to take responsibility for the doctor's appointments to stay abreast of health conditions changes. Or you may take the social outings to help you and your family member maintain some of the fun aspects of your relationship. This is the time to consider your boundaries. Clearly communicated boundaries are required so that your family member's loss of freedom does not significantly impact your freedom. It may be uncomfortable to see your parent in pain, refusing all options but your services. Still, tough love is required for the transition and a sustainable continuation of the journey.

Conversations

Discussions around driving were the most challenging series of conversations I faced while on this journey. The conflict highlighted an overarching theme of the entire experience until I understood the dynamic. In the beginning, it was a battle for control. Who was in charge? Growing up, Dad was the gentle enforcer, and I was mostly obedient. I was not prepared nor interested in swapping these roles, and neither was Dad. I was not parenting a child, but what was this strange new relationship, and what were these strong uncomfortable emotions? We were both resisting our new roles and responsibilities.

After recovering from a stroke at 94, when Dad came home from rehab, he demanded his car keys. I said, 'No way.' He turned all shades of red, then purple, and demanded that I give him the keys, made threats. For the first time, I understood the term "spitting mad." I lost all resolve. I was fearful that he was going to have a heart attack or another stroke. I needed him to calm down and gave him the key. I was shaking, angry, furious, lost, and afraid. He finally relented and agreed not to drive. One day, I used Dad's car and as I turned the ignition, Sinatra blared from the radio at a volume only Dad could tolerate. I demanded to know why he had been driving when he promised he wouldn't. He demanded to know who told me. Then, he said he had his fingers crossed when he promised not to drive. He remembered that he had hidden a spare key under the car.

Kathy Blair from KRB Move Management stated the reality well, "Children who hire us to help move their parents often have two personas: one when dealing with us and another when their parents are present and part of the conversation. When dealing with us, they are decisive, self-assured, and competent. In the presence of their parents, they are compliant, apologetic, emotional, and sometimes fearful. Often, there is a cry for help, sometimes spoken and frequently implied, 'Please take this burden from me.' We have been told, 'You don't know what he can be like. I don't want to see his wrath.' We totally understand this."[46]

When I let go of outcomes, I was able to release the anger and fear. I had fulfilled my responsibilities, communicated concern, enlisted the support of professionals, and set up alternative transportation options. I set boundaries around my emotions. I acknowledged that I owned the worry and the obsession with anticipatory guilt, therefore, these anchors were mine to set free. When I became aware of my thoughts drifting to driving, I took a few deep breaths to focus on the present. Through journaling, I further explored my frustration and identified a feeling of anticipatory guilt. I realized that the reason I felt alone was because no one else, particularly Dad, seemed to be as concerned as I was about what might happen, who could be injured, what consequences might be incurred. I was a lone paddler working against the current and it was wearing me out.

In addition to setting limits around my emotional investment, I set boundaries around my actions. I would not call the police and report that Dad was driving without a license. I did put a club on his vehicle and set a key aside for the aides. Dad still tried to drive the car with the club on the steering wheel, but with more curiosity than

---

[46] Kathy Blair, "Success cannot always be judged by the view from the corner office", *KRB Move Managers* (blog) September 26, 2019, https://krbmovemanagement.com/success-cannot-always-be-judged-by-the-view-from-the-corner-office/

determination. He eventually accepted that he would no longer be able to drive, and the club was no longer necessary. The strategies I employed to navigate the transition did not directly lead to the solution, but they helped me survive the emotional rapids that made me feel as if I were drowning. By accepting that I could not control Dad's behaviors nor the resulting outcome and by placing boundaries around my emotional involvement, I created a more sustainable experience. I protected my well-being so that I could continue to look after Dad's well-being. It was the best that I could do and it was enough.

11 OVERSEE MEDICATION MANAGEMENT: CHART A SAFE PASSAGE THROUGH PRESCRIPTIONS

Today I got my happy pills and my ticked off pills mixed up. I took one of each so now I'm ticked off but I'm happy about it.

UNKNOWN

AS A NEW caregiver, managing Dad's medications was one of the most daunting responsibilities I faced in the early days. I was certain that I could make a mistake that might result in Dad's death. This was not a completely unfounded fear. Each year 1.3 million people are injured by medication mismanagement.[47] 140,000 older adults die each year from taking prescription medication

---

47 Denys T. Lau, "Consumer medication management and error," *Clinical therapeutics*, 30, no. 11 (2008): 2156–2158. *https://doi.org/10.1016/j.clinthera.2008.11.010*

improperly.[48] Medication-related problems cause up to 30% of senior hospitalizations in the US.[49] It will serve you well to have a general idea of your parent(s) medicines before the information is needed. Ask the questions when the conversation is more casual, and you can approach the subject with curiosity.

An initial conversation can help you understand the current situation and alert you to any obvious issues. The first step is to understand what medications have been prescribed and why. A bit of research can inform you about side effects and possible drug interactions. It is helpful to know what supplements are added and the reason. You can research the side effects of any drug on the National Library of Medicine website. Drugs.com offers a tool to check for medication interactions and provides other important information, including how drug interactions occur and what other factors may cause interactions. The next step, which may happen in the same conversation, is to understand the frequency of each medication or treatment. This information will alert you to the level of complexity. What system is in place so that medications are taken as prescribed? Are they sorted into containers or taken straight from the bottle? You could

---

48 Diane Liga and Diane Litterer, "Promoting Wellness and Preventing Substance Use Disorders in Older Adults," *Behavioral Health News,* January 1, 2015, *https://behavioralhealthnews.org/promoting-wellness-and-preventing-substance-use-disorders-in-older-adults/*

49 Nibu Parameswaran Nair, et al., "Hospitalization in older patients due to adverse drug reactions -the need for a prediction tool," *Clinical interventions in aging*, 11, (2016): 497–505. https://doi.org/10.2147/CIA.S99097

ask what, if anything, gets in the way of remembering to take prescribed medicines. Over time you will want to look out for signs of missed doses such as pills on the floor, comments from your family member about missed medications, or symptoms that may be due to a missed dose. A possible sign of overmedication is running out of a prescription well before the next is due.

This initial conversation will help you set a baseline. You can periodically ask about changes, monitor concerns, and use awareness to determine when a change may be needed. You can begin to think about the next step that may be taken when the system is no longer working. There are many reminder services, devices, and apps to help manage the challenge of remembering to take medication. Knowing the options will help you and your family member collaborate and more smoothly transition to a more effective system when the time is right.

Getting Organized

Dad had been sorting and taking the pills on his own before having a stroke. Post-stroke, sorting became my responsibility, and it was time to get serious. I made a list of his medications and color-coded them based on morning, evening, and a blend of the two colors for the pills he took in the AM and PM. The list included the purpose, dosage, pill shape and color, quantity, and frequency. All that was missing was the phonetic pronunciation. I reveled in the reaction of the healthcare professionals when I handed them my project. I was organized, competent, color-coded. The lesson, yet to learn, was that that was the easy part of managing medicine. It was smoke and mirrors, the illusion of control. My color-coding gave me confidence, and at the end of the day, that was the real value. Following the request for a list of medications, the second and third most commonly asked questions were about hospitalizations and allergies. Hence, the back page of the medications list included Dad's history of hospitalizations. Allergies to medicines could be included as well.

I also recommend starting a binder of medical details, including a spreadsheet or log of physician and doctor visits. You can use this notebook to track symptom changes, medication changes, or any concerns, such as changing behaviors, that may help you identify patterns and help you remain aware of when more oversight would be helpful. The notebook is the perfect place to keep a list of doctors and contact information. You might include disease-specific details here as well for quick reference. If you attend doctor appointments with your family member, you can capture notes of the discussions during the visits. This could be a written note, but you may want to record the physician's conversations and instructions. An app called Abridge is a great tool to record conversations. It has a useful feature that identifies each medical term and provides a definition and information from a reliable source. It is helpful to have a recording as a reference when there are conflicts or confusion about what was said by the doctor. You may easily share the recorded information with family members reducing the possibility of transfer of information errors.

Communication and conflict
Compassion
It is helpful to understand why conversations around medication management can stir up emotions that seem out of proportion. It is difficult to empathize with our family member's accumulative loss that they may have incurred up to this point. They may have lost the ability to participate in hobbies and interests, travel, and they may have lost many friends and family members from their generation. Now, they face losing the capability to take their own medicine, something they have done for decades. This battle for control could reflect a much deeper fear. What's next? If I'm not capable of something so simple, what does that say about me? What will happen if I need to rely on someone else for my medications? It can be terrifying, but rather than fear, you may be confronted with anger, resistance, and an epic battle.

When you approach the conversation with compassion, conflict will be minimized. Consider the list of losses incurred by your parent and strive to help them maintain as much control as possible while you navigate this aspect of aging. Suppose you view the resistance as an attempt to remain relevant rather than a challenge to reason. In that case, the outcome will feel more collaborative. The conversations will be less stressful, and the transitions will have a reduced negative impact on relationships.

Words matter

When possible, start conversations with questions, listen, and be curious, in contrast to making accusations or posing accusatory questions. Attempt to understand your family member's perspective and express empathy. Repeat what you hear and ask clarifying questions as needed. Based on what you hear, choose words that convey a desire to give your parent control of the outcome. David Solie provides much insight into why conversations can be unnecessarily controversial in his book, *How to Say it to Seniors: Closing the Communication Gap with Our Elders*.[50] When we don't understand what is behind the resistance, our words often incite fear and anger. This book should be required reading for all adult children of aging parents. It is a handbook of skills and simple strategies such as using certain verbs over others. When we re-word requests and suggestions using the verbs recommended by David Solie, it gives control to our family member. Use verbs such as control, direct, guide, lead, choose, and manage.[51] For example:

> **How Not to Say It:** "Dad, your pillbox is a mess. Some daily pills are missing, and others are added twice. It's time for me to take over your medicines."
>
> **How to Say It:** "Dad, I understand that mistakes are going to happen. How can I help you

---

[50] David Solie, *How to Say it to Seniors*
[51] David Solie *How to Say it to Seniors* 152

so that you can continue to manage your medications? Think about it and let me know what ideas you have."

This response creates space between the discovery that your parent has missed taking medicines and your reaction. It allows your parent to maintain dignity and gives them an opportunity to be involved in the solution. When you revisit the subject and listen to their suggestions, you will be seen as a collaborator rather than someone trying to take control. You may agree to try one of your parent's suggestions or have a few ideas of your own to offer.

Another strategy is to be curious. When your parent rejects your suggestions, you might ask, "You seem hesitant to make a change in how you manage your medications. What is your greatest concern?" Several conversations may be required, but when you continue to be curious, listen to the response and keep the lines of communication open, your efforts often lead to an outcome that will benefit you both.

Sorting and Systems

After the stroke, Dad accepted and appreciated that I kept his medications straight, considering that prescriptions had changed, and his mind was still fuzzy. When he was ready to return to his sorting role, he wasn't just insistent, but adamant that he take over. Like driving, medication for both of us represented independence. I dreaded the day that he could no longer manage his medicines. If he could no longer take them from a pill container, what would that mean for our collective freedom?

Low vision and poor dexterity eventually made sorting too tricky for Dad. Sorting medications is a task that cannot be delegated to a caregiver aide but can be done by a registered nurse (RN). There are several pill sorting devices, from simple weekly containers to automated dispensing devices. Because Dad wanted to maintain as much control as possible, and Joe and I took trips that sometimes lasted weeks, I sorted Dad's medicines into a 32-day pill container. It was a project, but when done, Dad was able to manage the process. Joe and I were able to take mini trips with the addition of aides who helped out 9 hours a week. Then, Dad decided that he could make improvements to the system. One day, I noticed that the boxes were unordered, days mixed up, and half were flipped upside down from day to night. Pills were also out of place in half of the 31 boxes. It looked like it took a lot of effort to reorder and reimagine this new scheme.

Dad was not interested in a conversation about what had happened or why. The system was no longer working because Dad was no longer happy with it. He requested to try sorting on his own again. I left him to his work. Pills were doubled up on some days and missing from others. I would continue to do the sorting, but the 30-day container was no longer an option. We transitioned to a pharmacy that pre-sorted the pills. Dad reluctantly accepted and successfully converted to the new system.

If you think this might be a viable option for your situation, I recommend researching the national and local pharmacies that offer pill sorting. To better understand the difference in services and each option's benefits, you might call with a list of questions. Ask how a mid-month change in prescription will be handled. It is essential to find the right fit. If you are not happy with the service or the customer service, try another pharmacy. Sustainable caregiving involves a lot of trial and error. It may be significant work to change, but the right pharmacy will help make the change go smoothly. You will likely still use a drug store pharmacy that is open on weekends to supplement unique needs, such as medications taken as needed and medicine to treat temporary conditions such as a urinary tract infection.

Side effects

As you become more involved in medical details and become a care collaborator, you may begin to question if all the medications taken by your family member are necessary. Considering side effects and drug interactions, could less be more? Discuss the options with the primary care physician to gain more insight into recommended medication or dosage changes as a person ages. Drug store pharmacists are also a fantastic source of information and guidance. A local pharmacist shared a useful tip. She said that Saturday and Sunday, late afternoon, was a very slow pharmacy period and the perfect time to get extra help and advice, often with undivided attention. The pharmacist was the ideal resource when I was unsure how an over-the-counter medicine might interact with Dad's prescriptions.

Making Changes

Regarding making changes to a medication regimen, Dr. Gerardo Moreno, Associate Professor and Interim Chair of the Department of Family Medicine at UCLA, advises caution, "I think a caution for patients trying to reduce the number of prescribed medications is that they should talk to their doctor first before making any changes…But also [patients should] ask their doctor to make sure that they are taking indicated, evidence-based medications that are shown to improve their long-term health outcomes."[52]

Dad took nine prescription pills, and five doctor recommended supplements. This was a bit more than the average senior living at home but closer to the average taken by a senior in a nursing home. During each visit to the doctor, I asked that we re-evaluate the mix of medications to determine if we could eliminate any of them. The doctor was reluctant. Dad was 98. The mélange was working. But was it? There is little guidance for when

---

[52] Michael O. Schroeder, "How to Safely Reduce the Medications You Take", *US News & World Report*, May 28, 2015, https://health.usnews.com/health-news/patient-advice/articles/2015/05/28/how-to-safely-reduce-the-medications-you-take

to stop a medication. Not only are some medications unnecessary in older adults, but they may also be unsafe. Dad was in favor of reducing the number of pills he took, but he was not a fan of the process. Tapering and trial and error needed to be managed by a physician and the results closely monitored. At one point, we eliminated one of Dad's medications, modified another, and considered starting the process to reduce one more. The key to safety was to have the conversation and coordinate with Dad's physician.

Joan Baird is the director of pharmacy practice with the American Society of Consultant Pharmacists. She cautions, "Because older adults metabolize (break down) medications more slowly, drugs can hang out in their body longer, and a drug that might make a younger person feel slightly tired the next day could leave a senior lightheaded when they get out of bed."[53] Benadryl was one of the many over-the-counter options that we needed to avoid. The main active ingredient, diphenhydramine, caused trouble and was hidden in plain sight in many other over-the-counter medications. I became more vigilant and kept a list of ingredients to avoid on my phone so that I could quickly check labels. We also shared this information with Dad's caregivers who took him shopping. When he requested a sleep aid, they helped him make safer choices.

---

53 Lisa Esposito, "How to Help Aging Parents Manage Medications", *US News & World Report*, August 22, 2014, https://health.usnews.com/health-news/patient-advice/slideshows/how-to-help-aging-parents-manage-medications

Mishaps and Mismanagement

Minor mishaps, such as unknowingly dropping pills, can be a signal that more assistance is needed. Occasionally, we found tablets on the floor. We brought it to Dad's attention without making it a big deal, just to reinforce that he be careful. His response was often, "How the heck did that get there?" said with absolute incredulousness. We learned to toss the fallen pill immediately into the trash. Otherwise, he would ask to see it, take it for a closer look, and put it into his mouth. The evidence was gone, so it never happened. A neighbor found a pill on the floor and put it on the table. He swallowed it before she could say, "Noooo!!". The look on her face was priceless. This did not happen often, but the first time, I overreacted and madly tried to figure out what he had taken to determine if I needed to call Poison Control.

Similarly amusing was Dad's response when we asked what happened to a morning or evening's pills taken in error. He sincerely did not know where they could have possibly gone and was genuinely as surprised as we were that they were missing. Eventually, the mistakes became too frequent. Dad forgot that he took his morning meds and took them twice. Then, he took his nighttime meds in the morning. That was a quiet day, other than the snoring.

It was time for tighter controls. We considered an automatic dispenser but never entirely bought into that solution. Instead, we purchased sauce or condiment cups so that we were ready for the next step. After more significant mistakes were made over several weeks, we had the conversation with Dad. It didn't go well. He got quite angry at the suggestion that we set out his meds in a cup in the morning and again in the evening. He suggested another solution. I was doubtful but agreed. He put the nighttime container next to his bed and left the daytime container on the coffee table. Unfortunately, that went off the rails within a week. On two occasions, he took his nighttime meds twice and once did not take his daytime meds until we checked it later in the day. It was helpful to have logged the mishaps because Dad did not believe that the mistakes had been made, and he was quite convincing. If I had not kept a record, I would have questioned my memory.

It was a tough transition. We were not in a happy place for weeks. Dad said he wouldn't take his pills if he couldn't have it his way. I said, "No problem." We would set the meds out morning and evening, and he could take them whenever he wanted or not at all if that's what he chose. Dad scrunched up his face and said some out-of-character, unkind things, "What's wrong with you? You're enjoying this…" He asked me if I was trying to get revenge for something he did during my childhood. He had already forgotten the mistakes he made when we separated the daytime and nighttime meds and honestly thought we were unreasonable and spiteful. His words could have been hurtful, but they washed over me, not penetrating my heart. This part we just had to endure, wait it out, stay calm, stand firm.

Curiosity helped me keep perspective. How much of what he said would he remember? Would he apologize? Would we repeat the confrontation later that day, then again, the next day? Would he accept the change and not discuss it again? All of these were possible. I held my phone and recorded as we were talking. I was talking. He was yelling and putting his hand up when I started to speak. I hoped to assess if I could have handled the situation better. I could have. As I was watching, I saw his desperation, inner turmoil, and pain.

It was vital for me to remember that Dad was an accumulation of all of his experiences, not this one moment of resistance, anger, and emotion. Joe, Dad, and I all played a part in getting us through this adjustment as smoothly (or not) as possible. Dad's participation was framed by the losses he had already experienced as he worked his way to 99. He had given up tennis, golf, travel, *driving*. Over the years, he had lost those closest to him; his wife, friends, classmates, and shipmates. His eyesight and hearing were severely diminished. We brought him his meals and delivered supplies from his lists. Dad remarked once that Amazon must be quite a store. He appreciated our help, but it was not how he preferred to exist, relying on someone else, making a list, and then handing it over.

Each of these losses represented a chip at his dignity, and this latest one was a chunk. His disbelief wavered between two inconceivable truths. First, the knowledge that we believed that he was not capable of taking medicines from a pill container. And second, the realization that he was not capable of taking pills from a pill container. Either way, the anger, fear, and resentment that he felt must have been overwhelming. Those emotions matched the anger, fear, and resentment that I was feeling. The difference was that it was my responsibility to get us through this with love and hopefully be able to look back with some laughter because laughter is, indeed, the best medicine.

Boundaries and Mindfulness

Reinforcing boundaries was another key strategy that helped me navigate the conflict. Saying no to Dad, no matter how positively I phrased it, felt disobedient. It brought up feelings similar to those I remembered when I disappointed, displeased, or failed to be "good enough." It felt like I had time traveled and was back in that rebellious teenage stage. The day-to-day dynamic and discord created by this battle for perceived control affected my confidence and emotional health. When I realized that I was allowing Dad's anxiety to permeate my well-being, I reinforced emotional and physical boundaries. I stopped taking on his pain and disengaged from conversation as soon as it turned adversarial. Eventually, the waters calmed, and Dad accepted the new system.

Boundaries and mindfulness went hand in hand like two people in a peaceful relationship. Being mindful of the reason I felt anger or anxiety, mindful of when a boundary was crossed, allowed me to respond rather than react. Mindfulness created the space between my reaction and action. It helped me not only to identify the crossed boundary but gave me time to take a break and choose the right words. Mindfulness helped me focus and visualize what a win-win outcome might look like in each situation. "Begin with the end in mind," became the mantra that guided our united path forward to safe and effective medication management.

12 | PREPARE FOR CARE AT HOME: TRAIN FOR TURBULENT AND SWIFT WATER

Life is like the river, sometimes it sweeps you gently along, and sometimes the rapids come out of nowhere.

EMMA SMITH, *ENGLISH NOVELIST*

GETTING HELP IS a foundational piece of the sustainable caregiving puzzle. It is not an easy decision because there is much research and preparation required before providing care for a family member at home. Before committing to providing care at home, you will want to determine if it is financially feasible. Who will provide care and are they trained? While some responsibilities and tasks require training, and it will require research to locate the best resources, training can also take place in impromptu situations. For example, if you are in the hospital and the nurse or tech is about to perform a procedure or is sharing information, ask if you may use your camera to record the process or gather details. If home health care therapists are working with your family member, learn what you can so that you may continue the work beyond scheduled therapy. Is special equipment needed? How will medication be managed? To understand the help that will be available, begin to research agencies that provide medical and non-medical care.

I wasn't prepared to manage the responsibilities following Dad's hospitalization. No one responsibility was too challenging, but when all the tasks and responsibilities were combined, the work was all consuming. One minute I was floating along in the raft, and a minute later, I was out of the raft and in over my head. I felt submerged by conflicted emotions. I did not want this responsibility. I wanted to live my life as I had been accustomed, responsible for our small team of two. Guilt permeated the layers of emotion. A family member said, "Caring for someone is not a burden when it is family." A burden is exactly how I described the experience in my journal. Never out loud until her words took my breath away. It sounded like justification for not showing up, leaving the responsibility to me. I challenged her statement, "It is a burden."

Catholic upbringing instilled guilt deep into my fiber and the fibers were twisted and tangled into knots. I felt guilt for saying it out loud, guilt for feeling conflicted, guilt for wanting Dad to move from his home so that he was no longer our burden, guilt for feeling that Dad was a burden. When I shared that I felt guilty, a therapist told me that I had done nothing wrong, and I should not and could not feel guilt for a thought or a feeling. In response, I felt guilt about feeling guilt. I did not want this responsibility, but I took it. I took it but did not accept it. The conflict that I felt between what I was doing and how I was feeling was torture until I gained new perspective, and moved to, through and beyond acceptance. I reached a new reality and I physically and metaphorically wanted to be in this caregiving space.

For some caregivers, it may be a disease diagnosis or simply a slippery slope of accumulated tasks and responsibilities that leads to an unsustainable situation. Mired in resistance, we resist the reality of our fate and resist the help that will move us to a more sustainable existence. When we accept our circumstances, we often see the value in accepting help. Receiving the right help is like grasping the life preserver.

When Dad returned from rehab after the stroke, I took over more tasks and responsibilities than I could handle. With minimal research and a neighbor's recommendation, I selected a home care agency. The reviews weren't great, but they weren't great for any of the options, and I decided that only the dissatisfied clients wrote reviews. The aide who would assist Dad was a poor fit, but we didn't have time to "try out" more options. She was loud and abrasive and talked more than she listened. When I calculated the worst that could happen, it wasn't that bad. But I calculated wrong. We lost our beloved cat and learned a painful lesson. Don't rush the process, research and reviews matter.

I made a second attempt to locate and select an agency. I spent more time reading websites and reviews, including reading between the lines. I chose one and met with the representative who happened to be the owner. He stayed for two hours and learned about Dad and our situation. He and his wife had a very personal care story and reason for starting the business. He shared information that helped me understand the dynamics at play when the person receiving the care was resistant to outside help. He said the key was to find the right person who clicked with Dad.

Altogether, we worked with this agency for five years. It wasn't all calm waters, but each time we reached the rapids, the agency staff tossed us a lifesaving buoy. In the beginning, after a few attempts, we found the perfect aide match, and when they clicked, as predicted, Dad looked forward to her arrival. I called it "match dot com" for the care recipient, family caregiver, and paid caregiver. Having strangers in the home was not comfortable, but in the end, the benefits outweighed the discomfort.

When you find the proper assistance, you can begin setting up a framework that will support you through the duration of the experience. Lightening your caregiving load will free up some of your time to plan for the inevitable and unexpected events. These plans will empower you. You will have more time for self-care and can prioritize your well-being. Concerns about your family member can crest and feel like a raging torrent that sweeps you away from the present moment. While you may minimize worries in other areas of life, in caregiving, it is helpful to face them head-on. Awareness will prompt you to make plans for the "what ifs." Having a plan will enable you to focus on moving forward rather than ruminating on what might happen or dwelling on the past. For example, what would happen if you could no longer take care of your loved one? Who could step in, or how might the transition into a care facility transpire? You might meet with a care facility representative and talk through every detail of what might unfold. I had a plan in place in the event that a hospitalization led to a permanent move to a care facility. Once this plan was in place, I could more clearly focus on care at home.

If you choose to hire an agency, you will work with a representative from the agency to establish the scheduling and care provided. Working with an agency versus hiring a private aide may appeal to you considering the following benefits:

- The agency staff receives training and must stay current on certifications
- The home care agency has insurance to cover mishaps
- The caregivers have cleared background checks (Verify that the agency conducts national background checks as well as state investigations.)

- Taxes are paid by the agency rather than paid by the care recipient or family caregiver
- If an aide can't fulfill the shift, another aide will fill the gap
- The agency can offer direction to the aide and handle performance concerns that may arise
- You do not need to locate paid caregiver candidates

But, sometimes, hiring a private aide is the best option. Many areas in the country are not supported by an agency, and it might be necessary to locate one or more individuals to help with care. You can turn the list of needed services into a reverse resumé. List the qualifications that are required and maybe a bit about your family member's hobbies and interests. From here, you can begin to hand them out to a church, hospital, senior center, or other agencies that employ or are in contact with staff or volunteers who help seniors.

Your care recipient might be resistant to having someone in the home, might not accept that help is needed, or disagree with how assistance is provided. Therefore, it is crucial to identify an aide or aides who will be a good match for your loved one. For example: a loved one who likes to chat might prefer a more talkative aide, and the reverse is true; a quieter experience may be preferred. Someone interested in the same hobbies could be a great match, e.g., painting, gardening, puzzles, etc. If your family member enjoys home-cooked meals, an aide who likes to cook may appreciate the opportunity to share their talents in the kitchen. You might begin by having the aide simply do light housekeeping and some meal prep. Once a relationship is developed, your family member will likely be less resistant. When the right match has been made, your care recipient might even look forward to the visits. If your loved one's resistance is still a challenge, you might appeal to your family member's concern for your well-being. Share that you need help helping them.

A few steps will help you narrow down the care options and begin the research. First, identify the type of services you will need and what type of agencies provide these services. There are two types of care agencies with similar names, and it is important to know the difference. One is home health care which offers "skilled care" services, and the other, home care, which offers "non-medical care" services. Non-medical care does require skill and training, but not the same training as a nurse or therapist. Here is a breakdown of the fundamental differences between these two agencies.

Home health care services require a doctor's orders and provide temporary assistance, usually following hospitalization or injury. The services are designed to help the patient regain independence and are provided by a nurse and possibly one or more therapists. Home care agencies provide personal care services including help with Activities of Daily Living known as ADLs. These are non-medical and considered foundational to independent living. They include: dressing, bathing, toileting, eating and moving from one spot to another. Aides from these agencies may assist with light housekeeping. Homemaker aides help with Instrumental Activities of Daily Living known as IADL's. These are non-medical activities, important to independent living, but not critical and include light housekeeping, preparing meals, grocery shopping, running errands, laundry, companionship, and medication reminders. Home care nurse services may include: administering medication and injections, monitoring vital signs, wound care and other medical therapies.

List the services that you need. Think about the conversation and possible questions as you begin to prepare for the meeting or phone conversation with an agency representative or private hire candidate. For example, consider whether you would like transportation to be included in the services and if so, whose vehicle would be used the aide's or your family member's? Will your family member require help with ADL's or more companionship-type services? Will the agency work with you on matching an aide who is a good fit with your situation both for needs and personality? What training is provided for the staff? What background checks are conducted prior to hiring? Will pet care be included? How does the communication process work so that you will be able to stay informed about care and concerns? Then, you are ready to do the research. Get referrals, recommendations and read reviews. Understanding your needs and wishes will help you determine if the agency or individual is a good fit.

Once you understand your parents' wishes and have determined the care that is needed, you can consult with an elder law attorney to ensure that any financial steps you take are not in violation of Medicaid or Medicare guidelines. There are many specialty areas under the Elder Law umbrella, so it is crucial to find the attorney who best fits your requirements. Locate an Elder Law attorney at the National Academy of Elder Law Attorneys or get a referral. Meet for an initial consultation to determine if the attorney is a good fit for your family and your situation.

Whether you are working with an agency or have hired a private aide, it's not easy having new folks in the home and communication will minimize the frustrations that might arise. If something is being done in a way that makes you uncomfortable, start with questions to better understand the reasons. Then ask yourself if the outcome is acceptable. The aide's process may be a different way of accomplishing the same objective. Letting go of control doesn't mean letting go of standards. While we might feel that we are the best caregivers, we can also acknowledge that others are very effective at providing care, and we do need their help.

Effective communication is key to ensuring that you profit from the additional help. A notebook to share notes back and forth could work well to communicate questions, answers, concerns, and new information. A daily or weekly checklist may help everyone stay on track. Texting or phone calls may be the preferred way to communicate. No matter the method, the important thing is to keep each other current, and if you have more than one aide helping with care, it is even more critical that the communication is consistent. Communication with family members also requires strategies. Regularly scheduled family meetings might be the best avenue to keep everyone up to speed. Technology is also an option. Some apps allow you to log in and share a family member's medical information, track appointments, medications and share other information with family members and the care team.

Another option for managing care is to turn all duties over to an Aging Life Care Professional® (previously known as a geriatric care manager) who will take responsibility for overseeing all care needs. This comprehensive service runs about $100-$250/hour with the objective to safely help your loved one age in place while maintaining a certain level of independence. Services include assessing needs, creating individualized care plans, coordinating, and overseeing care. Some agencies provide a host of other options such as managing finances, nutritional counseling, help with family conflict and additional services that complete a well-rounded package. This is an excellent option for providing care for a loved one from a distance or if your situation does not allow you to be involved in full-time care.

Paying for in-home care can present a challenge. Consider speaking with an elder law attorney and a financial advisor who is familiar with elder issues. Family members may be able to pool personal financial resources and provide care or a combination of options may help cover the costs. If your family member is a veteran, two programs may help finance care, Homemaker and Home Health Aide Care[54] and Aid & Attendance.[55] The local Area Agency on Aging is a public agency that exists to help people age in place. They provide and share local and regional resources that include homemaker assistance, meals, respite services, and more. Information on services can be found at *https://eldercare.acl.gov*. If your loved one has a Long-Term Care Plan, take some time to read and understand the eligibility requirements. You may enlist the help of the underwriter or an elder law attorney to decipher the details.

Palliative care and hospice care are other levels of care to understand because it is often misunderstood and can be of great help to you and your family member. Palliative care is designed for symptom management following a diagnosis of a serious illness. A team including doctors, nurses, and other health care professionals provides comfort care through an organized program. Palliative care

---

54 "Homemaker and Home Health Aide Care," *US Department of Veterans Affairs*, accessed June 14, 2020, https://www.va.gov/geriatrics/pages/Homemaker_and_Home_Health_Aide_Care.asp

55 "VA Aid and Attendance benefits and Housebound allowance," *US Department of Veterans Affairs*, accessed June 14, 2020, https://www.va.gov/pension/aid-attendance-housebound/

may be covered under an individual's private insurance. In contrast, hospice services provide an array of helpful services when a diagnosis of a terminal illness has been given. Care is designed to manage symptoms and enable the care recipient to remain at home and maintain quality of life for as long as possible. The services include coordinated care to address the care recipient's physical, emotional, and spiritual needs and needs of the entire family. Typically, but not always, life-prolonging treatments are declined when a patient is in hospice care. Care may be provided at home or in a care facility. When a patient qualifies for hospice, care is most often covered under Medicare but check your family member's policy to be sure.

What other community and private support and services are available to help lighten the caregiving load if your care recipient is being cared for at home? Many communities offer a Meals on Wheels program, a service that can be sourced through your local Area Agency on Aging. Grocery, produce or paid meal delivery services may be options. Amazon offers several subscription and delivery services to facilitate ordering and reordering food and other staples. So many options! It can be confusing to know and decide what will work best in your situation. Research the options, try one or a combination, decide yay or nay, repeat. What public and senior transportation services might allow your family member more freedom and give you a break from the chauffeur role? Some care facilities offer the opportunity for a temporary stay which gives you a chance to get a bit longer respite. There may be a minimum stay requirement, such as 30 days, making the option less attractive if you are looking for a one or two-week vacation option. Of course, it would be possible to pay for the 30-day stay and only take advantage of the time needed.

Adult day centers offer an opportunity for your loved one to get out of the home, bond with other clients and staff, participate in a program that may involve exercise, crafts, or other activities, and have a meal or two. It is an opportunity for the family caregiver to get a break and some centers offer support resources. Not all adult day centers offer the same activities and socializing opportunities. Similar to when deciding on the best home care options, start by identifying your needs so that you can narrow down the choices. Some day-center programs cater to seniors with physical or memory-related disabilities. The center's description on its website or in printed materials offers initial guidance to help determine if the activities and interaction would be a good fit for your family member. Have questions ready when you visit. Check cleanliness, coziness, friendliness, adequate staff. Are the clients engaged in activities? What type of medical attention is available if needed? Some day-centers provide help with showering and grooming. Does your loved one have special needs to accommodate? A trial day or half-day may be offered to see if the center is a good fit for your family member and if your family member is a good fit for the center. If your family member does not bond with the other members or connect to the activities, check into other centers. This solution does not work for everyone. The only way to know if it will work is to try.

There is fear in the unknown. We don't know how long we will be on this journey on the caregiver river, the winding curves we will experience, or the depth of the challenges we will face. However, we can use these challenges to motivate us to learn and find a better way forward for us, our loved one, and our care team. The turbulence and waterfalls hold a power, grace, and vitality that lead to rainbows, which is the nature of the caregiver river.

ACKNOWLEDGMENTS

I began writing this book while I was caring for Dad. I wanted to help fellow family caregivers who were struggling as I had. I wanted to give them hope and tools to create their own meaningful and sustainable caregiving journey. Family caregivers were my inspiration, and they fueled my purpose and passion. Dad passed away three months after I turned the manuscript over to my editor. It was unforeseen, and the void was immense. As family caregivers continued to reach out for support, they were throwing me a lifeline as well. This book is my gift to the caregiver. I hope that it will guide them to navigate their caregiver river with confidence.

Chandra White-Cummings is a talented editor who understands the challenges of caregiving firsthand. I appreciated Chandra's guidance and insight. She helped me connect the sustainable caregiving strategies with my personal caregiving story in a way that fulfilled my vision.

Denise M. Brown, the owner of the Care Years Academy, was my teacher and mentor when I began my pursuit to support fellow family caregivers. A repository of caregiving wisdom, Denise made sense of what seemed like a chaotic experience. What I learned from Denise gave me the confidence to chart my way forward as an advocate for caregivers.

Linda Burhans, The Gal Who Cares for Caregivers, was an inspiration to me when I was caring for Dad and continues to be a shining example of how to make the world a better place for caregivers. Early in my caregiving experience, I read Linda's book Connecting Caregivers: Answers to the Questions You Didn't Know You Needed to Ask. I highlighted sections and dog-eared pages. After founding Sustainable Caregiving, I met Linda, and she graciously accepted my gratitude and admiration. I appreciate her continued support and friendship as we collaborate on our shared mission.

Most of all, I want to thank my husband Joe, my rock and co-caregiving partner. Caregiving is a rite of passage, and for us, it was a couple's rite of passage. Joe was a problem solver, an empathetic ear, and a companion in all things fun. Our relationship grew stronger during the seven years that we cared for Dad. I watched Joe and Dad develop a bond that comes from mutual respect and am grateful that they had this time together.

www.ingramcontent.com/pod-product-compliance
Lightning Source LLC
La Vergne TN
LVHW021711060526
838200LV00050B/2601